Critical Acclaim for
Same-Sex Marriage? A Christian Ethical Analysis

"A must read for anyone who wants to take an informed position on this issue. Marvin Ellison's book offers an essential voice in the marriage debate by bringing the broad ethics of Christianity to what is otherwise a legal question about the justness of discrimination against gay and lesbian couples in civil marriage. He takes to task all the players in the debate, and brings to bear the rich justness and compassion of Christian ethics to enrich the debate."

— Mary L. Bonauto, Civil Rights Project Director for GLAD
(Gay and Lesbian Advocates and Defenders), lead counsel in
the *Goodridge v. Dept of Public Health* case in Massachusetts,
and co-counsel in the *Baker v. State of Vermont* case

"Unlike most Christian theologians Marvin Ellison refuses to oversimplify the complex social and moral questions facing us in the area of human sexuality. This is a brilliant book, filled with fresh insight on topics that usually pall when addressed through the lens of conventional wisdom. In it, both Ellison and the work of Christian liberative ethics shine."

— Carter Heyward, Howard Chandler Robbins Professor of Theology,
Episcopal Divinity School, Cambridge, Massachusetts

"In the vortex of a vigorous, often acrimonious, public debate on the subject of same-sex marriage, Marvin Ellison brings a note of sanity, good will, and grace. Refusing to engage in bifurcated arguments that demand a firm, often unthinking, 'yea' or 'nay' on same-sex unions, Ellison calls for what he terms 'sexual justice.' This is not just a demand for Christian reformation — essentially for a new gospel of understanding the importance and multiplicity of sexual pleasure: 'good news about sexuality and sexual difference.' It is a call for common sense and common justice in how we, as a culture, must allow, promote, and sustain a wide range of intimate relationships. Written with energy and argued with elegance, Ellison's book will be a revelation to everyone who cares about society, families, love, sex, politics, and justice."

— Michael Bronski, author of *The Pleasure Principle:
Sex, Backlash and the Struggle for Gay Freedom*

"Don't be fooled by the title of Marvin Ellison's new book! It is indeed a well-researched, lucid, probing, and thoroughly informative discussion of the same-sex marriage debate, an admirably succinct analysis of the social and moral arguments put forward by theological and legal voices. But it is much, much more! Most important, it is the first book-length study that challenges intellectually honest people, especially Christian people, to cut through the rhetorics of fear to look at how our marriage perspectives can be recast to offer genuine moral wisdom. Reshaping discussions of the theology of marriage, in ways that hold out hope that Christians might contribute positively to social policy discussions on the changing world of family structure and intimacy, is no small feat given pathological fear on the issue that grips many Christians.

"The additional really good news is that Christians can recommend this small book as good marriage theology to friends who have given up hope that churchly teaching on these issues will make sense. And women, including self-respecting feminist women, can read it without having to cringe at the typical theological evasion of male theologians about marriage as the site of theological injustice, violence, and social control of women's life. In fact both 'marriage traditionalists' and ardent advocates of gay marriage badly need the book. The former can learn why their efforts are leading in policy directions very different from what they intend. The latter can learn to consider how their ardor may obscure many questions that need attention in forming a defensible alternative theological position. Failure to heed Ellison's call for a deeper visioning of how both religious communities and the state address this question will leave us the poorer in both religious and political contexts."

— Beverly Wildung Harrison, Professor of Christian Ethics, Emerita,
Union Theological Seminary, New York

"Heterosexuals have no monopoly on love, and Marvin Ellison brilliantly shows in this book that the right to marry is a human right, not an award for being heterosexual."

— Daniel C. Maguire, Professor of Moral Theology,
Marquette University, Milwaukee

"Ellison's treatment of marriage for LBGT people parallels that of Catholic feminists on women priests: the traditional institution is so morally flawed that access to it is of dubious value in the present, despite the fact that it is a too-long delayed right. His thoughtful and persuasive call is for: (1) a reformation of marriage as a public as well as personal relationship that should serve justice to all women and men; (2) a Christian de-centering of sex and marriage; and (3) a recognition of the diversity of human sexualities."

— Christine Gudorf, Professor of Religious Studies,
Florida International University, Miami

"This book is a much-needed primer for Christians who are trying to stake out a decidedly Christian moral approach to same-sex marriage. Ellison offers a clear and probing use of legal scholarship that is especially helpful to Christians who may not have thought about the web of moral assumptions embedded in our marriage laws. Besides Christians, it is a "must read" for anyone interested in furthering their understanding of our society's deep anxieties about the public and private morality of sex and marriage for lesbians, gay men, bisexuals, and transgendered persons, as well as for heterosexuals."

— Traci C. West, Associate Professor of Ethics and
African American Studies, Drew University, Madison, New Jersey

"The daring and veracious voice of a leading Christian ethicist who offers clarity and hope in the swirling opinions over same-sex marriage. Marvin Ellison's queerying of sex, marriage, legal and Christian traditions through the norm of justice/love is stellar! He asks the salient questions: Why is marriage controversial? Which changes should be encouraged or resisted? For what reasons? And for whose likely benefit or loss? With elegant and intelligent prose, Ellison scrutinizes the troubling and 'peculiar' debate and constructively combines social justice and religious convictions to help sort out 'conditions for sharing life among intimates, and more broadly, among diverse social groups.' Read, teach, share this book — for insight and courage to join with others shaping publicly cogent and morally persuasive stances."

— Marilyn J. Legge, Associate Professor of Christian Ethics,
Emmanuel College of Victoria University in the University of Toronto

"This book could not be more timely. Ellison takes the reader on a provocative, engaging search for an ethical understanding of same-sex marriage. His brilliant analysis will help lead us to the day when the freedom to marry — as well as the freedom not to — will be available to all, regardless of sexual orientation or gender identity."

— Debra W. Haffner, Director, Religious Institute on
Sexual Morality, Justice, and Healing, Norwalk, Connecticut

"Marvin Ellison gets it right in this welcome book, refusing to be drawn into a simple 'yes/no' debate on same-sex marriage. He recognizes that what is at stake is not adding more couples, albeit same-sex couples, to the privileged status of marriage. Rather, cultural and religious struggles over marriage, all marriages, are an opportunity to do justice. De-centering marriage and re-centering justice-love is the task at hand. He illuminates it thoroughly and points a faithful way."

— Mary E. Hunt, Women's Alliance for Theology, Ethics and Ritual

SAME-SEX
Marriage?

A Christian
Ethical Analysis

MARVIN M. ELLISON

THE
PILGRIM
PRESS
Cleveland

To Frank

Life partner and lover of justice

The Pilgrim Press
700 Prospect Avenue
Cleveland, Ohio 44115-1100
pilgrimpress.com

© 2004 by Marvin M. Ellison

Printed in the United States of America on acid-free paper

09 08 07 06 05 04   5 4 3 2 1

Library of Congress Cataloging-in-Publication Data
Ellison, Marvin Mahan.
    Same-sex marriage? : a Christian ethical analysis / Marvin M. Ellison.
        p.   cm.
    Includes bibliographical references.
    ISBN 0-8298-1560-0 (cloth. : alk. paper)
    1. Marriage – Religious aspects – Christianity. 2. Same-sex marriage – Religious
aspects. 3. Same-sex marriage – Law and legislation. I. Title.
BV835.E46 2004
241'.63 – dc22
                                                                    2003062423

Contents

Acknowledgments

THIS PROJECT has its origins in two pleasurable occasions, the first an invitation to contribute an essay for a special issue of the *Union Seminary Quarterly Review* in honor of Professor Beverly Wildung Harrison. For those who have been inspired, as I have, by Bev's life and work as a feminist liberation ethicist, it will come as no surprise that a topic like same-sex marriage becomes an opportunity for reflecting on the meaning of justice. The second occasion was participating in a panel discussion on marriage reform at the University of Southern Maine with Evan Wolfson and Mary Bonato, two leading legal theorists and social activists in the freedom to marry movement. Engaging in interdisciplinary work with them and other visionary intellectuals in the legal community has been nothing short of a delight.

My graduate assistant, Angie Buxton, trained in both law and theology, helped me early on to gain access to the legal literature. Professor Jennifer Wriggins at the Maine School of Law provided law review articles and met for lively conversation. Librarians Beth Bidlack and Linda Ronan at Bangor Theological Seminary came to my rescue more than once.

A group of colleagues, including an attorney, a historian, an Episcopal priest, two therapists, a theater director, and a community educator, met with me twice during the writing of this book to discuss my ideas — and press their own — about marriage, intimacy, social change, and sexual justice. I am grateful for their wisdom and support, so my thanks go to Sally Campbell, Lisa Difranza, Michael Dwinell, Meredith Jordan, and Howard Solomon. Beverly Harrison and Charlene Galarneau read various chapters and encouraged me to claim my authority. Anne Underwood deserves special commendation because she read the entire manuscript and made constructive suggestions on almost every page. I'm grateful for all their advice and only wish I had followed it more closely.

Faculty colleagues at Bangor Theological Seminary responded with their characteristic enthusiasm and insight about this project. The seminary's Board of Trustees, with the encouragement of President William Imes and Dean Glenn Miller, provided generous funding for a 2002–3 sabbatical leave. Speaking engagements at Emmanuel College of the University of Toronto and Middlebury College gave me opportunities to refine some of my thinking, and I am grateful for the hospitality extended to me by Michael Bourgeois and Marilyn Legge and by David Edelson and Johanna Nichols.

Timothy Staveteig and Ulrike Guthrie at The Pilgrim Press are the kind of publisher and editor that every author should have.

Elizabeth Ellison, my sister and beloved friend, let me know at crucial junctures that non-LBGT people also need this book.

This case study in ethics makes its appearance only because of the remarkably courageous LBGT rights and liberation movements. I am amazed by and grateful for LBGT people everywhere who claim their right to love and be loved, including those who desire to marry, those who don't, and those who will never be granted the choice.

Frank Brooks, my life partner, read numerous drafts, listened with a discerning ear, and cheered me on when energy flagged. Above all, he helped me appreciate, on a daily basis, that loving requires work and play, but not necessarily a marriage license. For these reasons and more, I dedicate this book to him.

A Peculiar Debate

We need to be
changing the questions.[1]
— ADRIENNE RICH

S AME-SEX MARRIAGE[2] is a hotly debated topic. On the one side, a spokesperson for Pat Robertson's Christian Coalition speaks of same-sex marriage as society's "greatest challenge" because it "directly attacks the family." Lou Sheldon from the Traditional Values Coalition warns that extending equal marriage benefits to gay couples will represent "the degendering of America."[3] On the other side, gay activist Gabriel Rotello argues that acquiring the legal right to marry will be the "single greatest victory in all of gay civil rights," so much so that it is "difficult to overstate its importance."[4] Similarly, E. J. Graff in *What Is Marriage For?* describes same-sex marriage as "a breathtakingly subversive idea" because it celebrates the shift toward seeing sex as "justified not by reproduction but by love."[5] To complicate matters, others within the LBGT community question whether the right to marry should be pursued at all. Still others propose the abolition of marriage as a state-sanctioned institution.

Within this complex swirl of opinion, Christian faith communities have, by and large, not contributed in a positive way to furthering the conversation or resolving the conflict. Typically, the religious response has been reactive ("just say no") or conflict avoidant ("just say nothing"). Many public policy advocates and social activists presume that religion rejects homosexuality outright and that religious people are opposed to marriage for same-sex couples. Even more troubling, while legal scholars have brought a moral seriousness to these issues by offering sophisticated ethical justifications for their positions, much

Christian theology with respect to these issues is embarrassingly thin, as if Christians do not believe they need to develop publicly cogent, morally persuasive arguments about such matters.[6]

A call for interdisciplinary ethical inquiry

As a corrective for this deficiency, throughout this study I intentionally converse with legal scholars as well as theologians, in part because lawyers are among the most morally informed on this topic, and in part because too many Christian commentators fail to draw on other disciplines to sharpen their moral sensibilities and arguments. Legal theorists, historians, and social theorists may help theologians (and religious people, more generally) to gain deeper appreciation of how the institution of marriage as a multicultural phenomenon is not so much "breaking down" as it is, once again, changing. For their part, theologians may remind others that religion will inevitably play a role, one way or another, in the resolution of this contest. After all, religion deals with how communities, in binding people together through the sharing of stories and ritual, prioritize certain values and give shape to distinctive visions of the good life. Religion, too, is a multicultural phenomenon that is not so much "breaking down" as it is, once again, changing.

This book provides an ethical analysis of the current debate about same-sex marriage in the context of profound cultural change. My conviction is that both religious and nonreligious claims about family, sexuality, marriage, and intimacy should be subject to ethical scrutiny and continually evaluated in terms of our wisest, most informed convictions about what promotes the good of persons, the strengthening of community, and the care of the earth. The salient questions to ponder are these: which changes should be encouraged or resisted, for what reasons, and for whose likely benefit or loss?

What is missing from, or at least underrepresented in, the marriage debate is an ethical analysis that is explicitly progressive *and* informed by religious conviction. By progressive, I mean an ethical stance that is gay-positive, supportive of same-sex partnerships and families, and committed to honoring marriage and other ways in which people create intimate relationships and sustain diverse kinds of families. By a progressive religious perspective, I mean one that places justice making at the heart of (in my case, Christian) spirituality and views marriage, sexuality, and family through a justice lens, asking how to set wrongs right and establish a fairer distribution of power, authority, and goods within diverse communities.

Because of pervasive sex-negativity within the Christian tradition, a major revision of Christian ethical teaching is called for, not only about marriage but, more generally, about human sexuality and intimacy. In an earlier work, I noted that, historically speaking, the Christian tradition has never had a constructive ethic of sexuality that truly affirms the goodness of bodies, welcomes the gift of sensuous pleasure, and honors the rich diversity of human sexualities.[7] Rather, because of its devaluing of sex, body, and women, Christianity has developed a more circumscribed *marriage ethic* that has designated only heterosexual, marital, and reproductive sex as morally legitimate. Christianity and other religious traditions are being pressed to incorporate fresh insights from the natural and social sciences and, above all, to reconstruct their teaching in light of newly found wisdom from grassroots movements for gender and sexual justice. Increasingly, people are fed up with a fear-based ethic of sexual control and are challenging the church, from inside and outside, to come of age about sex, marriage, and family life. A serious reform of Christian ethics is needed to honor human sexual diversity and energize people to resist sexual exploitation and oppression. This book seeks to contribute to this larger project.

This broader renewal movement toward gender and sexual justice gives ample reason for turning to the topic of marriage. As Rita Brock explains, "By the end of the twentieth century, most Christian churches, Catholic and Protestant, had acknowledged that sexism was a sin. They have not, however, scrutinized one major social institution perpetuating sexism — marriage."[8] I agree, but find even this assessment incomplete. By and large, the church has also failed miserably to repent of its oppression of LBGT people. The same-sex marriage debate provides an opportunity, first, to scrutinize how the politics of marriage within religious traditions has perpetuated both heterosexism and sexism and, second, to explore how best to repair the damage.

Ethics from conflict

Ethical inquiry emerges out of conflict. In this society conflict is particularly intense about sexuality, gender relations, and family. Those distressed over the loss of "traditional family values" have sounded an alarm about moral slippage and social decline. Many others find themselves confused about shifting cultural attitudes toward sex and uncertain about how to move forward. From all sides there is an acute awareness of a cultural crisis with respect to sexuality and family life. For at least the following reasons, marriage has become a flashpoint of controversy.

First, marriage is controversial because *marriage* is the most revered and conflicted of cultural institutions. It encompasses, among other things, economics, property, reproduction and childrearing, caregiving, and extended family and community relations.

Second, marriage is controversial because it requires talking about *sex*, a stigmatized subject and major source of cultural anxiety. Even though this culture is saturated with sexualized imagery, most people maintain silence about "intimate matters" or at least refrain from speaking about them publicly. Marriage is the culturally designated place for tucking sex away within a zone of marital privacy.

Third, marriage is controversial because the institution is about the *regulation of sex*, as well as love and intimacy. Same-sex marriage presses questions about whether marriage should be exclusively heterosexual, whether "good sex" is necessarily heterosexual and marital, and whether same-sex love (and sex) can be holy and, therefore, should be supported, protected, and blessed by the community.

Finally, marriage is controversial because even though the institution has served some people well, it has fostered *gender and sexual oppression*, including the oppression of women and LBGT people.

About marriage, I enter into this debate asking, what recommends marriage to begin with, making it ethical and worth entering into?

What would a progressive Christian ethic look like that commends marriage as a site for bonding and deep human intimacy, yet does not regard marriage as the only site for living responsibly as a sexual person? What would it mean to *decenter marriage* and not grant it privileged status?

About sex, my question is, what would it mean to *decenter heterosexuality* and not grant it privileged status? What would a progressive Christian ethic look like that regarded homosexuality as a morally good way to be and "do" sexuality? What difference would it make to focus moral concern not on gender and sexual identity, but on the quality of relational intimacy and whether our connections with one another are just and compassionate? What would it mean to recognize a plurality of human sexualities — bisexuality, intersexuality, transsexuality, asexuality, homosexuality, and heterosexuality — and honor all persons by respecting the diversity of ways in which they live and love?

About sexual justice, my question is, what if the institution of marriage no longer enabled the control and repression of human sexuality, especially women's sexuality? What if marriage no longer stigmatized and excluded people because they were judged too queer to be "the marrying kind"? What if marriage were regarded as a site, for gay and non-gay people alike, to learn how to deepen mutual pleasure and strengthen the bonds of human affection and solidarity? What would it mean to shift away from the dominant Christian ethic of control that teaches fear of sex and move toward a progressive ethic of empowerment that encourages people to enjoy sex and live comfortably with their own bodies, alongside sometimes radically different bodies? If all this were the case, would marriage still be recognizable as marriage? Would this ethic be recognizably Christian, or does that matter? These questions will be explored in the chapters to follow.

A heated debate, full of irony

This discussion should alert the reader to the fact that people have strongly differing opinions about marriage, including lesbian and gay marriage. That clash of viewpoints, along with the intelligence and passion with which people express them, makes this debate heated. What makes it peculiar is that lesbians and gay men are among the most conflicted about whether marriage is a desirable personal goal or should be a community priority. On the marriage question, the LBGT community is deeply divided.

Regardless of how people view this topic, few anticipated that same-sex marriage would produce such contentious debate in the United States Congress, in state and federal law courts, or within religious traditions. In 1996 Congress rushed to debate and quickly passed the "Defense of Marriage" Act (DOMA). This legislation defines marriage, for the purpose of federal laws and programs, exclusively as a union between a man and a woman. It also gives states the authority not to recognize same-sex marriages from other jurisdictions.[9]

Ironically, DOMA was hastily enacted to "defend" marriage even though not one state legislature, the source in the United States of family and marriage law, had moved to grant marriage to same-sex couples. Since 1996, thirty-five state legislatures have adopted similar DOMA statutes, allowing them to deny legal recognition of gay marriages contracted in other states.[10] These laws have clearly been enacted for a single purpose: to exclude lesbians and gay men from exercising a civil right that other adult citizens freely exercise in marrying the partners of their own choosing.

Shortly after the federal DOMA was signed into law by then President Clinton, Chris Glaser noted another irony in a *Newsweek* guest column: "I've lived long enough in the gay movement to witness those who oppose us come full circle in their reasons that we should be outcasts from church and society. Twenty years ago, gay love was opposed because it supposedly didn't lead to long-term relationships and the rearing of children. Today gay love is attacked because gay people in committed relationships and gay couples with children are coming out," and even seeking to marry. In the past gay men and lesbians were castigated for being selfish, promiscuous, and irresponsible. "Now we're denounced," Glaser writes, "if our selfless service — from the ministry to the military — is revealed." Within his (and my) denomination, the Presbyterian Church (U.S.A.), lesbians and gay men have been declared unfit for ministry "because we didn't form lasting relationships," and yet, when someone in response to these complaints dared to "mention the possibility of sanctioning gay marriages, audible gasps came from the crowd. We could *talk* about gay ordination," Glaser points out, "but marriage was more sacrosanct!"[11]

Given that marriage is a loaded issue for many people, including religious people, it is wise to unpack the multiple parts of the same-sex marriage question. First of all, what role, if any, should the state have in relation to same-sex relationships? Legal scholar Carlos Ball puts the question this way: "Does society have an obligation to recognize and support the relationships and families of lesbians and gay men?"[12] Should two gay men be allowed to enter into civil marriage and have their union recognized by law? Second, what role should church, synagogue, mosque, or any other religious institution have in relation to same-sex relationships? How can faith communities enhance the lives of nonheterosexual people and strengthen their intimate partnerships? Should two lesbian women receive a religious blessing of their committed partnership and be publicly recognized as married "in the sight of God"? Third, if same-sex couples were to gain only one option, either civil marriage or religiously solemnized unions, which would be more significant? Finally, who should have definitional authority over what counts as valid marriages and "real" families?[13]

It is at such moments of uncertainly and conflict that ethical inquiry is called for, when basic matters are in question and it is no longer possible to take for granted what should be done, undone, or left alone. Although engaging a contested social question is never a smooth and easy process, I wager that undertaking an ethical appraisal of this debate is timely and worth the effort. After all, negotiating the conditions for sharing life among intimates and, more broadly, among diverse social groups is always a matter of moral importance, sometimes even with life-and-death urgency, as some contestants to this debate argue. My hope is that this book will be of value in sorting out these matters and showing how a justice-centered Christianity can be helpful for getting to a far different and better world.

A roadmap for this inquiry

Chapter 1, underscoring marriage as a changing and changeable institution, looks at definitions of marriage and examines some of the historical and cultural changes regarding this most treasured and contentious institution.

Chapter 2 proposes the benefits of viewing the same-sex marriage debate through a justice lens, informed by insights from progressive religious and social justice movements.

Some readers may wish to skim these initial chapters, skip them entirely, or return to them later in order to jump ahead to the three central chapters, which discuss the same-sex marriage debate in detail.

Chapters 3, 4, and 5 address, in turn, how marriage traditionalists, advocates, and critics define the issues and frame their arguments, respectively, in opposition to same-sex marriage, in support of extending marriage rights to lesbian and gay couples, and in favor of dispensing with marriage altogether.

Chapter 6 asks how the Christian tradition might contribute to justice making for LBGT people and others.

Chapter 7 makes a case for rethinking both civil and religious marriage from a progressive Christian ethical perspective and concludes with reflections on justice and love.

As I write these words, I am mindful of several recent historic events and of a momentum that appears to be building. Belgium has officially joined the Netherlands in granting full and equal marriage rights to same-sex couples. In early June 2003, an Ontario appeals court ruled that Canada's ban on lesbian and gay marriage is unconstitutional.[14] Shortly after the decision was announced, an Ontario Superior Court judge presided at the civil marriage ceremony of Michael Stark and Michael Leshner, the latter a longtime legal activist for ending the Canadian marriage exclusion. A ruling is also expected soon from the Massachusetts Supreme Judicial Court whether that state will become the first in the Union to issue marriage licenses to same-sex couples. A similar case is pending in New Jersey.

In late June 2003, the U.S. Supreme Court in *Lawrence v. Texas* struck down anti-sodomy laws while declaring that the state has no interest in banning private, consensual sex between two men or two women. Lesbians and gay men, like their heterosexual counterparts, have a constitutionally protected right to privacy in intimate relational matters and, in Justice Kennedy's words, are "entitled to respect for their private lives." "The State cannot demean their existence," the ruling continues, "or control their destiny by making their private sexual conduct a crime."[15] In a sharply worded dissenting opinion, Justice Scalia counter-argues that when a majority believes that certain sexual conduct is immoral, that belief provides ample reason — and a "rational basis" — for governmental regulation of that conduct. Because this historic Court decision may eliminate the legal basis for distinguishing between different-sex and same-sex unions, Scalia even questions whether approval of same-sex marriage may be next on the Court's agenda, an outcome he opposes.[16]

Given the fast pace of change, these and other developments may render outdated some of the factual claims in the pages to follow. At the same time, I doubt that the main lines of argument about same-sex marriage will change all that much or that the heat and excitement that surround this topic will end any time soon. Therefore, I trust this book will have ongoing value as this debate continues.

That said, I also must pause and ask whether this or any book calling for more study is really needed. After all, similar calls for "more study" have been invoked in the past merely to delay change whenever the demands for justice could no longer be ignored. Therefore, the reader must decide whether this present inquiry is an aid or a hindrance for the "great work" of our times, the extension of justice as rightly related community. For myself, my hope is that this book will enlighten people about this most "peculiar debate" and draw attention to the possible contributions of a progressive Christian ethic. Even more, I pray it will spark action and hasten the day when a truly comprehensive justice is more fully realized.

CHAPTER ONE

Marriage Changes

> The only certainty — and of this we are sure —
> is that couples will continue to form and reform
> throughout the next millennium.[1]
>
> — LAURA L. CARSTENSEN AND MARILYN YALOM

I N APPROACHING THIS TOPIC, it is wise to maintain both historical perspective and cross-cultural awareness that marriage is neither changeless nor unchangeable.[2] A historical sensibility is especially needed to offset claims by self-described traditionalists who refrain from using a historical method. This tendency was apparent during the United States Congressional debates regarding the Defense of Marriage Act. A Republican senator cautioned his colleagues against tampering with an institution that he asserted had remained the same during "five thousand years of recorded history." Another senator, this time a Democrat also speaking against altering marriage policy, appealed to "thousands of years of Judeo-Christian teachings" and to "the true definition of marriage" as "eternal."[3]

Despite such ahistorical claims, marriage as an institution has assumed a variety of forms and served purposes quite different from those familiar to contemporary North Americans. Christian ethicist Gloria Albrecht, in her recent study of women's work and U.S. family policies, models an ethical method that emphasizes how marriage and family patterns are bound up with, and deeply affected by, prevailing economic and political conditions.[4] For this reason, marriage, family, and sexuality must be carefully placed in historical and cultural context. Otherwise, we might miss taking into account an insight that informs all social change movements: the way things are is not the way things must be. Whatever is can be undone or at least modified through collective human agency.

To place the current conflict about same-sex marriage in context, I begin by looking at the politics of regulating marriage. The legal right to marry has never been available to all groups in the United States. Religious tradition and customs have also forbidden some unions. I then consider some current demographic changes, especially the decline of what is often called the traditional nuclear family — a husband-provider and wife-homemaker with dependent children at home. Sociologists and other theorists speak of the emergence of a postmodern family because there is no culturally dominant marriage or family pattern. Indeed, a multiplicity of options competes for people's loyalties. After a brief sketch of United States marriage and family history, I consider definitions of marriage and the distinctions between civil and religious marriage and between marriage as a relationship and as a status. Reviewing these definitional, political, and cultural shifts will set the stage for analyzing in subsequent chapters the various parties to the same-sex marriage debate.

Marriage regulations

By all accounts the decision about whom to marry, as well as whether to marry at all, is one of the most momentous decisions a person can make in her or his lifetime. Although parents, friends, and even opinionated strangers may want to dictate who marries whom, the state itself takes a "hands-off" stance by not interfering with a person's choice about such a highly personal matter. More accurately, the state *appears* to be neutral in allowing people the freedom to select a life partner. The truth of the matter is that marriage is also a political as well as a personal act. Throughout U.S. history, some classes of people have run up against the coercive power of the state whenever they have fallen in love with a person of the "wrong" race or gender. Interracial marriage was illegal in many states until the late 1960s. In the not too distant past, women were not regarded in law as "marriage equals" to their husbands. Therefore, when it comes to interracial marriages, women's equality within marriage, and more recently same-sex partnerships, the state has been anything but neutral and noninterfering.

Regarding even intraracial heterosexual unions, the state has long stipulated eligibility requirements although these regulations are surprisingly few in number and set only minimal expectations. In almost all states, the two people in question must be at least eighteen years old (or acquire special permission), not be close blood relatives, not be presently married, pay a small fee, and pass a blood test.

The limit on age is designed to meet two needs: first, to prevent the "sale" of young girls and other acts of coercion, and second, to discourage marriages between persons considered too young to understand (and, therefore, fulfill) the obligations of a marital commitment. Restrictions against marriages between blood relatives have sought to avoid abuses of power within close family relationships and to protect the health of offspring. Rules limiting marriage to only two people at a time seek to protect women because, as Michael Wald explains, "a person [read: man] married to several persons [read: women] will not be able to adequately assume the economic obligations of marriage (including those that arise in the case of divorce)." Also, multiple partner arrangements are considered less likely to produce satisfactory intimacy and emotional growth over the long haul.[5] In addition, the state requires an authorized agent (a judge, justice of the peace, or clergyperson) to officiate at a public ceremony. The couple must declare before witnesses that they freely consent to marry each other. A marriage license must be properly signed and registered with the state.

All things considered, civil marriage is not weighed down by state regulations and is entered into rather easily. Perhaps more accurately, marriage is entered into easily if a person is heterosexual and has fallen in love with a partner of the other sex. If a person seeks to marry another person of the same sex, legal obstacles are quickly encountered. In fact, the vigor and haste with which the restriction on same-sex unions is enforced is noteworthy, given that the state places such minimal restrictions on marriage and takes little notice of other differences, including the couple's religious affiliations and economic status. By singling out lesbian and gay couples, state restrictions send a message that single-sex bonding is so wrong that it calls forth the state's coercive powers.

Marriage laws have reinforced other restrictions that later have been identified as unjust and oppressive. As early as 1705, a Massachusetts law was enacted to ban interracial couplings. By the end of the nineteenth century, at least forty states had similar laws forbidding people from marrying a spouse of the "wrong race." The California courts were the first in the nation to declare an interracial marriage ban unconstitutional, but that ruling was handed down only in 1948. Because of the unfettered power of Jim Crow segregation at the time, the decision was widely denounced as threatening the stability of Western civilization. As one Southern judge argued,

> Almighty God created the races white, black, yellow, malay and red, and he placed them on separate continents. And but for the interference with his arrangement there would be no cause for such marriages. The fact that he separated the races shows that he did not intend for the races to mix.[6]

This judge and other defenders of the status quo invoked a divine mandate to ward off critique and bolster a racially constructed institution. However, as E. J. Graff points out, "You can tell that the anti-reformers were losing when they started insisting that any change would bring down God, Nature, and civilization." When these are declared at stake, it is a safe bet that "change is on the way."[7]

Even with reform underway, it took nearly twenty years after California lifted its ban on interracial marriage before the United States Supreme Court struck down the remaining state statutes that rendered marriages between different-race couples illegal and subjected the spouses to criminal prosecution, typically for fornication. In its historic 1967 *Loving v. Virginia* decision, the Supreme Court declared marriage one of the basic "personal vital rights." Furthermore, the freedom to marry belongs to all citizens. By so ruling, the Court sought to reinforce the value of marriage as a stabilizing social institution. The free exercise of this marriage right, the Court noted, is "essential to the orderly pursuit of happiness by a free people."[8]

Because the right to marry is considered basic to personal identity and necessary to promote the social welfare, in 1987 the U.S. Supreme Court took another step to protect the rights of yet another class of citizens. This time the Court struck down a restrictive state law that prevented prisoners from marrying. In its decision, the Court described marriage as a human right and defined its essential features as follows:

- an expression of emotional support and public commitment;

- for some, an act with spiritual significance, and for some the exercise of a religious faith;

- a relationship with the expectation that for most, the marriage will be consummated; and

- a relationship that can receive tangible benefits, including government benefits and property rights.[9]

As the Court underscored in its *Turner v. Safley* decision, marriage is such an important social institution that even convicted felons ought not to be deprived of the freedom to marry. By extension, the Court's logic has protected the right to marry for other groups, including "deadbeat dads," the multiply divorced, and people who show no particular aptitude for married life but nonetheless seek the state's recognition and protection when they wish to "tie the knot."

Currently, the most noticeable exception to state noninterference in marriage is the denial of marriage licenses to same-sex couples. While these couples may seek and receive the blessing of at least some faith communities and be recognized as married "in the sight of God," when it comes to civil marriage, it is a different matter. In every U.S. jurisdiction, lesbians and gay men are denied the freedom to marry the person they love and with whom they choose to spend their lives. A legal advocacy group describes the situation this way: "Today, same-sex couples are not allowed to marry legally in any state — no matter how long they have been together, no matter how committed their relationship, and no matter how much their families need the protections, benefits and responsibilities that come with civil marriage." As they conclude, "This discrimination based on sex and sexual orientation is the last vestige of discrimination in marriage."[10]

Marriage changes

Marriage at the beginning of the twenty-first century is different from marriage as it was lived a century or even a half-century ago. For one thing, marriages do not typically last a lifetime. The average length of a first marriage is eight years and five to six years for remarriages.[11] For another thing, cohabitation is increasingly common for heterosexual couples prior to marriage and for divorced people prior to remarriage. In a study of contemporary North American couples, two social scientists emphasize that cultural attitudes about sexuality, procreation, and marriage have shifted considerably in the past century. "Fewer wait for marriage to experience sex," they observe, "and many do not consider marriage a prerequisite for bearing children."[12] In the early 1930s, only 8 percent of first births occurred outside wedlock; by the early 1990s, that number had risen to 41 percent. Although some first-time mothers marry their partners during pregnancy or soon after the birth of their child, this pattern of having children and postponing marriage (or not marrying at all) suggests that marriage is no longer a prerequisite for having children. Moreover, the desire for children is no longer the primary reason that people marry.[13]

Although in the United States a large percentage of heterosexual couples marry, the divorce rate is high. Research from 1996 indicates that approximately one adult in four goes through a divorce (24 percent). Contrary to stereotype, evangelical and fundamentalist Christians divorce on average at a slightly higher rate than the rest of the population (30 percent and 27 percent respectively).[14] Nearly one-third of all marriages are remarriages.

During the past thirty years, family size has declined (from an average household of 3.14 people in 1970 to 2.62 in 2000). At the same time, the proportion of households consisting of a married couple without children has remained fairly stable throughout this period (30 percent in 1970, 29 percent in 2000). What has changed dramatically is the proportion of households consisting of a married couple with children (40 percent of all households in 1970, 24 percent in 2000), in part a reflection of the aging baby-boomer generation with "empty nests."

Family patterns also vary according to race and ethnicity. In 2000, among the white or Euro-American population, 83 percent of all households were married-couple households. Among African Americans, less than one-half of households were married-couple households (48 percent), compared to 68 percent for Hispanic and 80 percent for Asian and Pacific Islander households.[15]

Nowadays, the marital family is no longer culturally dominant. A 2001 U.S. Census Bureau report, "America's Families and Living Arrangements," identifies several additional changes since 1970. The number of one-person households has grown significantly. The proportion of single mothers has increased (most notably among white women). More young adults are postponing marriage and living more years as single persons.[16] The median age at first marriage has risen for both men and women. Between 1970 and 2000, the proportion of young adult women, ages twenty to twenty-four years, who had never married doubled (from 36 percent to 73 percent).[17] A multiplicity of marriage and family patterns coexists. "The traditional nuclear family in America is dead," writes Richard Quebedeaux, "and no one knows for sure what will replace it."[18]

Historical overview

In the past, during periods of social and economic upheaval, supposedly fixed and divinely mandated marriage and family patterns have been dramatically overhauled. Given globalization and massive cultural disruptions within the United States and elsewhere, it is likely that the early twenty-first century will also witness significant transformations, continuing a process of change that was evident even at the beginning of the nation. Colonial households within a predominately agrarian society integrated economic, social, political, and cultural aspects of life. The interests of wives and other family members were subordinated to corporate family interests as defined by (and under the authority of) the family's male patriarch. Although stable in appearance, even these families experienced considerable flux. As one social theorist has noted, "Death visited colonial homes so frequently that second marriages and blended households composed of stepkin were not uncommon. Conjugal love was a bonus, not a prerequisite of such marriages."[19]

In the nineteenth century, the rise of industrial capitalism precipitated a massive reorganization of family patterns. Personal life and productive, wage-earning work were split into the separate spheres of a female-dominated private world and a male-dominated public world. In this gender-dichotomized world, women's work was devalued as it became less visible. First among the affluent and then among middle-strata whites, adult women and their children became increasingly dependent on the earnings of a husband/father laboring outside the home. During this time, the purpose of marriage began to shift. In an entrepreneurial age of expanding commerce, although procreation and extended family connections retained significance, marriage became redefined as a contract between two adults who pledged to build a life together on the basis of conjugal love and desire for companionship. Marriage was no longer "overseen," as it had been in colonial America, by extended family, church, and community. Rather, marriage became the couple's own private decision, an intimate project they managed on their own. As the world of (white, affluent) women was increasingly privatized, their lives became narrowly circumscribed by their domestic roles as nurturers of children and caregivers for their husbands. A "good wife" was needed at home to create for her husband a safe haven from the fiercely competitive male world of capitalist economic expansionism.[20]

By the early 1950s, three-fifths of North American households conformed to this husband/breadwinner and wife/full-time homemaker model. However, even as this modern nuclear-family pattern became prevalent after World War II, it represented only a transitional household pattern that never became the universal "traditional" family model idealized by the religious Right. Beginning in the 1960s, marriage and family patterns again shifted. The most noticeable change has been the decline in the proportion of U.S. households consisting of two married adults with biological offspring. By the 1990s, upward of 80 percent of heterosexual couples were cohabiting prior to marriage.[21]

A report detailing demographic shifts in U.S. families notes other changes. In the early 1970s, 72 percent of adults were married, 9 percent widowed, 6 percent divorced, and 13 percent never married. Three-quarters of underage children lived with both parents. A quarter century later, the demographics looked very different. In 1998, less than half of all adults were married (48 percent), about the same number were widowed as in the early 1970s (10 percent), nearly one-fifth were divorced (19 percent), and almost one-quarter of all adults had never married (23 percent). Slightly over half (52 percent) of children lived in families with both parents present.[22] In 1999, the U.S. Census Bureau reported that more than one-third (35 percent) of adults between the ages of twenty-five and thirty-four had never married. Among African Americans in this age group, more than half (53 percent) had not married.

While these demographic figures indicate a decline in the proportion of the population that is married, North Americans still show a persistent interest in marrying and creating households. In the year 2000, nearly three-quarters of men and women were married by their thirty-fifth birthday. By age sixty-five, about 95 percent will have married.[23] These statistics have led demographers to conclude that "marriage is still very much a part of American life."[24] Although married couples with children no longer constitute a majority of U.S. households, that change has occurred not because people are refusing to marry or form families, but for other reasons. One factor is economic. More single adults, including widowed older women and never- or not-yet-married younger adults, are able to afford maintaining a separate household. In addition, increased life expectancy means that more married adults will have finished raising their children and face a longer-term challenge as "empty nesters."

Other developments have had an impact on North American marriages and families:

- Increased urbanization (in two hundred years, the U.S. family has shifted from 95 percent rural to 97 percent nonfarm families).

- Demographic changes (increased life expectancy means more years of marriage after children are raised, so that a lifetime commitment to marriage is longer than in previous generations).

- Shrinking family size (in the late 1800s, an average family included between five and six children, plus two adults; in 1986, average household size was between two and three people).

- Increase in nuclear families (U.S. families are highly mobile, and extended families are spread across wide geographic distances).

- Separation of sex and reproduction (thanks to the development and mass marketing of safe and effective contraceptives, as well as legal access to medically safe abortion).

- Changing needs and expectations (marriages based more on personal and emotional fulfillment, less on survival needs, although this varies by class location).

- Changing views of marriage (marriage more as a personal contract negotiated between two parties, less as an institution sanctioned by organized religion).[25]

Two other changes should be included on this list: the increase in the rate of divorce (between 1970 and 1996, the number of divorces in the United States quadrupled[26]) and the expanding numbers of women in the workforce. "In 1975 a threshold was reached when 50 percent of the mothers of *school-age children* were active labor force participants. Another milestone was reached in 1980 when 50 percent of mothers of *preschoolers* worked outside the home. In the 1990s the 50 percent threshold was reached for mothers of *infants under one year* working for a wage."[27]

Contextualizing same-sex marriage

This book focuses on a marriage question that could only have emerged within a specific context. Debates about same-sex (civil and religious) marriage make sense in North America and Western Europe where LBGT people have gained sufficient visibility and legal standing to press for the right to marry. As noted earlier, there is nothing new about gay people enjoying significant friendships or forming intimate partnerships with members of their own sex. Even in the absence of social and legislative approval, they have done so in the past and will no doubt continue to do so in the future.

In 1998, the U.S. Census Bureau reported that among all the adult couples in the United States that were either married or living together, approximately 3 percent were same-sex couples. The percentage of lesbians and gay men living together as couples runs the same as the percentage of heterosexual couples living together, approximately 60 percent.[28] Other surveys indicate that, in self-reports about their primary relationships, most lesbian and gay couples in long-term, committed relationships think of themselves as "married." Somewhere between 30 and 50 percent have had a commitment ceremony, made vows, and exchanged rings. These ceremonies are frequently religious in nature and presided over by a clergyperson, an option in some Jewish and Protestant Christian traditions and under study in others.[29]

More speculatively, there is a long history of lesbians and gay men marrying their same-sex partners, as the late historian John Boswell conjectured in his study of early Christian marriage liturgies.[30] However, most often in the past when gay people married, they married a different-sex partner and, therefore, entered into marriage with varying degrees of willingness and success. What is novel today is securing the civil right — and religious blessing — to marry life partners of the same sex. Claiming the very same rights as heterosexual persons enjoy is one reason this debate is heated. (In fact, traditionalists insist that marriage by definition is a heterosexual institution and, therefore, barred to nonheterosexuals.) Another reason this issue is controversial is that marriage bestows status and privilege on those publicly perceived as marriageable.

Even a cursory glimpse at other cultures shows the enormous power of marriage to shape personal identity, confer social status, and determine the material conditions of people worldwide, especially women's welfare. A book entitled *Women in the Material World* describes a dozen married couples with quite differing experiences:

Bhutan: In a culture that has traditionally lacked formal marriage ceremonies, Nalim and her husband, Namgay, were considered married when he moved into her home; now they have been together for twenty years and have four children.

Jordan: Haifa Khaled Shobi and Ali Nawafleh almost didn't get married when Haifa's father, a Palestinian living on the West Bank, wanted to withdraw his consent; he couldn't bear the thought of his daughter living so far away. Ultimately, they were allowed to marry — the couple has five children.

India: Although Mishri Yadav's parents formally arranged her marriage when she was ten years old, she did not actually meet her husband, Bachau, until she was fifteen, when she moved into his house.

Mexico: Carmen Balderas de Castillo and Ambrosio Castillo Cerda did not marry until she was eighteen years old. She became pregnant at fifteen with their first child.

Ethiopia: To his current shame, Getachew Mulleta married Zenebu by abducting her from a village street — automatically forcing her parents to concede the match.

Italy: Although they believe that the formalities of state-sanctioned marriage have little meaning, Daniela and Fabio Pellegrini married after twenty years of living together because they wanted to give their daughter, Caterina, the legal recognition and protection afforded by a formal match.

South Africa: When Poppy Qampie became pregnant, she and her husband, Simon, got married — a source of some present-day ambivalence to Poppy, who feels that the early pregnancy interrupted many of the plans and hopes she had for her life.

Albania: Although Albanian tradition awards Hajdar Cakoni near-absolute power over his wife, Hanke, he thinks it wrong to control her; the couple shares the household tasks more than is usual in their village.

United States: After meeting at church, Pattie and Rick Skeen began dating when she was sixteen years old; they married when she was eighteen and still in college — earlier, she says now, than she will advise her daughter to do.

Japan: After her father died, Sayo Ukita realized that she would have to leave the family house, which was now the house of her older brother; perhaps as a result, she met and married her husband, Kazuo, within a year.[31]

Marriage is a cross-cultural phenomenon, and so, too, is the social change movement for extending marriage eligibility to same-sex couples. In 2001 the Netherlands became the first nation to recognize same-sex marriages *as legally valid marriages.* This European country no longer differentiates between marriages between a man and woman and those between two men or two women. Dutch public policy states, "A marriage can be contracted by two persons of different sex or of the same sex."[32] In recent years, other countries have passed similar national legislation, including Germany, France, Denmark, and Canada, although only Belgium has gone as far as the Netherlands. Nonetheless, each country recognizes and protects same-sex couples by offering various options, including domestic partnership, cohabitation rights, and reciprocal benefit partnership. In 2000, after the Vermont Supreme Court declared marriage discrimination on the basis of sexual orientation unconstitutional, the Vermont legislature enacted public policy that, for the first time in the United States, has legalized same-sex relationships under the rubric of civil unions. This legal status gives lesbian and gay couples the same rights, benefits, and privileges that heterosexually married couples enjoy, but without the name "marriage." (Civil unions also lack the portability that would require other jurisdictions to recognize a couple's union as valid under law. They also lack the federally mandated benefits accorded to spouses, including social security coverage for a married couple.)

Toward a working definition of marriage

In contrast to the brief cross-cultural portraits of marriage cited above, and despite the international momentum to modify marriage and family policy to accommodate lesbians and gay men, the definition of marriage provided by the *Westminster Dictionary of Christian Ethics* is terse, even bland. "Marriage," it begins, "is a joining of two lives." Two qualifications immediately follow. First, marriage is defined as "the voluntary union for life of a man and a woman." Second, although it is recognized that Christian norms and attitudes have shaped Western marriage in distinctive ways, it is conceded that Christianity does not have exclusive rights to marriage.[33] Moreover, to fully grasp the meaning of marriage, three interconnected aspects must be considered: the personal/relational, the legal/civil, and the religious/sacramental. While each dimension has importance, the emphasis varies according to who is consulted: heterosexual people who take marital privilege for granted as "everyone's" (read: their) right, lesbians and gay men seeking to change cultural norms and legal codes that deny them access to marriage, or the social theorists, public policy advocates, and religious leaders debating the pros and cons of same-sex marriage.

Among legal scholars and advocates, Evan Wolfson proposes to define marriage as "primarily a committed relationship of two people, recognized and supported by the state, who undertake a commitment and who receive important protections and benefits and also obligations and responsibilities."[34] He then adds two points, echoing the dictionary definition above. First, marriage is "the most important, most significant, most central social and legal institution in virtually every respect for most people." Second, the institution of marriage "is one of the most flexible, and yet one of the most enduring, human institutions" that has taken "many, many forms," and yet has lasting and "vital significance."[35]

Another legal scholar, John Witte, Jr., suggests tongue in cheek that marriage is "just a piece of paper." What is telling, to be sure, is what the paper signifies. If the paper is a marriage license, it has the power to make available over one thousand federal regulatory and statutory benefits and privileges, among them the rights of inheritance, decision-making capacity when a marital partner is hospitalized, the joint filing of taxes, adoption rights and spousal immigration status, and spousal social security and veterans' benefits. Access to this complex assortment of marriage perks is granted because marriage, Witte points out, is about entitlement. In fact, marriage is best understood as "a bundle of rights, responsibilities, privileges, and immunities that these two parties, this couple, have vis-à-vis each other and vis-à-vis the community."[36]

Historian Nancy Cott agrees that marriage should be viewed as more than a private arrangement between two people. Every legally recognized marriage requires a third party in the form of the regulatory state. Marriage is, therefore, both a personal relationship (Wolfson's "primarily a committed relationship of two people") *and* a public institution (Witte's "bundle of rights, responsibilities, privileges, and immunities" granted by the state). However, in order for a couple to *be* married, public recognition is required, not first and foremost by family, friends, or a religious community, but by the state. The state alone has the authority to enforce the couple's agreement as a legally binding transaction. In Cott's language, "Legal marriage requires state sanction." It is the public, through the licensing power of the state, that "sets the terms of marriage, says who can and cannot marry, who can officiate, what obligations and rights the agreement involves, whether it can be ended and if so, why and how."[37]

At this point a decisive distinction enters in between religious and civil (or legal) marriage. Insofar as a couple, whether same-sex or different-sex, is married but married only "in the sight of God," this couple is not married according to the regulatory authority of the state.

(This view will be contested in chapter 7.) As Wolfson acknowledges, "What counts legally is not marching down the aisle; it's the piece of paper that you sign in the vestibule, which says that you have a civil marriage license, which is the legal and economic institution."[38]

Religion and the politics of marriage

The shift in marriage regulation from church to state has been one of the most momentous historical changes concerning marriage. Even so, the role of religion is far from insignificant in shaping and giving legitimacy to the institution. In the United States, religion has promoted a very particular model of marriage: nonegalitarian marriage that is male-dominant and female-subordinate. Public policy has, therefore, not promoted marriage per se, but rather a very distinctive marriage paradigm, namely, "lifelong, faithful monogamy, formed by the mutual consent of a man and a woman, bearing the impress of the Christian religion and English common law in its expectations for the husband to be the family head and economic provider, his wife the dependent partner."[39]

Not surprisingly, a patriarchal Christian tradition has given its blessing to a patriarchal marriage paradigm. Moreover, the church has traditionally spoken of marriage not as humanly constructed but as divinely willed, mandated by scriptural authority, and expressive of the natural order of creation. Even a contemporary theologian highly critical of Christian patriarchalism writes in tones that reflect this longstanding religious investment in sanctifying marriage as if it were timeless and unchangeable. In *Marriage after Modernity*, Adrian Thatcher writes of marriage as "a universal institution which, theologically speaking, is given with creation itself (Gen. 2.24; Mk. 10.6–8; Mt. 19.4–6). It is written into the way things are." Pages later, he acknowledges "marriage is most obviously a historical institution which has changed through time. Indeed it may be misleading to continue to use the single substantive term 'marriage' as if there were a single, common, nuptial experience which can be discerned through history."[40] Thatcher's own slippage here, between language that suggests marriage is "fixed," "natural," and "eternal" and recognition of the historical character of marriage as socially constructed, should alert us to pay careful attention to how language is used and arguments framed.

Chapter 6 discusses Christian attitudes toward marriage and how they have changed. Theological conviction ranges from outright rejection of marriage as a Christian lifestyle, to a concessionary view that marriage is a "hospital for sinners" that constrains lust, to the more rhapsodic endorsement of marriage as "simply expected" of all adult believers. While it is true that, from time to time in the history of the church, theologians have praised companionate marriages, when they did so they had no intention of transforming the domestic order into something other than an arrangement between social unequals. Although the husband-father might be admonished to be a loving and responsible spouse, he would also be expected to be the one in charge. The wife fulfilled her Christian duty by being an uncomplaining "helpmate" and the mother of his children. Male leadership ensured good moral order. Given the power of marriage and family life to shape identities, roles, and expectations, marriage laws helped construct not only the household and family, but also the political order. Contrary to those who emphasize marriage as an exclusively *private* arrangement, marriage has always been *political*, as well.

Marriage shaped by gender, race, and class

As an institution rooted in sexism, marriage defines how men and women relate to each other within the family and beyond. Politically, marriage helps maintain a gendered social order, turning men into husbands/providers and women into wives/caregivers, assigning to them — and enforcing on them, through the apparatus of the state — differential status, roles, obligations, and, therefore, life prospects. As historian Cott summarizes, "The whole system of attribution and meaning that we call *gender* relies on and to a great extent derives from the structuring provided by marriage."[41]

Historically, the power of marriage to define gender relations has gone a long way toward establishing male control of women's lives (and bodies), especially as state regulations encoded male entitlements and privilege. Marriage has also been the lynchpin institution securing a sexist sex/gender order by fiercely controlling sexuality through the institutionalizing of heterosexuality. Heterosexuality becomes compulsory in at least two ways: first, by labeling as deviant (unnatural, immoral) and then punishing behavior that fails to conform to "normal" male and female gender roles and status, and second, by enforcing heterosexuality as the exclusive pattern for sexual relating.

One consequence of heterosexual marital exclusivism is that LBGT people are stigmatized as the deviant Other. At the same time, homoerotic intimacy becomes invisible and unthinkable because it lies outside marriage. Everyone is (presumed to be) heterosexually inclined. Erotic interest is supposedly sparked only by so-called "opposites attracting." Even for persons with homoerotic desires, loving another person like one's self becomes nearly or totally unimaginable, an erasure that is dehumanizing in its potency. Heterosexual marriage naturalizes as a biological mandate the exclusive pair bonding of differently gendered persons, one masculinized, the other feminized. Public policy upholds heterosexual marriage as the premiere site of normalized identity and status. Those barred from exercising the right to marry, a population that at times has included prisoners and the mentally retarded, are only further marginalized because they are seen as unfit to marry.

Marriage policy serves political functions. In the past it has legitimated white racial supremacy by barring slaves from marrying and interracial couples from marrying across the color line. Today it legitimates heterosexist exclusivism. Insofar as the institution perpetuates oppression, it is unjust. Whenever church and state endorse an unjust institution, the reputation of both religion and politics is tarnished.

Marriage as culturally constructed, concretely lived

Much contemporary legal discourse emphasizes marriage as an institution and downplays its relational aspects. The 1993 *Baehr v. Lewin* ruling, requiring the state of Hawaii to demonstrate a compelling interest for denying marriage licenses to same-sex couples, refers to marriage as a status conferred exclusively by the state. Regarding marriage as the state's creation effectively cuts marriage loose from Christian and other religious underpinnings or at the very least hides those connections.[42] The problem with this approach is twofold. First, it ignores the central role that religion has played in shaping marriage. Second, while it is not helpful to ignore the *political* character of marriage, it is also not helpful to lose sight of its *relational* significance for individuals and communities.

Although legally shaped, marriage depends, as Martha Nussbaum writes, on most people's "stated desire to live together in intimacy, love, and partnership and to support one another, materially and emotionally, in the conduct of daily life."[43] From a liberal human rights perspective, the state's role is to guarantee the conditions for human flourishing, including safety, economic security, and rights to free speech, association, and the pursuit (or not) of religion. Flourishing also involves the human emotions, especially the capacity to love and to be loved. Therefore, to be fully human requires actualizing the freedom to affiliate, which means concretely "being able to live for and in relation to others" and be treated as a person of worth.[44] The state's business should not be to regulate consenting adult relationships, but rather to protect the right of individuals to bond with intimate partners of their choosing — of whatever gender — without government interference or the state's approval or disapproval. Denying this associational right is disrespectful of persons and violates their personhood.

Marriage should also be viewed not as a private arrangement between two persons or as a "stand-alone" institution, but rather as a relational commitment that exists only within a web of wider social connections and obligations. A couple's relationship is deeply affected by the moral quality of the social order in which their marriage is situated, such that "there is a fundamental dialectic between the presence of a livable, humanizing community of persons and the quality of interpersonal intimacy and love which individuals can realize in their primary relationships." In other words, the quality of marriage as a personal relation is "derivative of and dependent upon the moral relations existent in the wider society."[45]

Ethically speaking, it is questionable to preserve marriage as a social institution without taking into account the quality of life this institution makes possible for actual people in actual marriages. Religious groups cause harm when they fixate on preserving the "sanctity of marriage" at all costs, requiring couples to preserve their marriages at the expense of their health, safety, and personal well-being. The negative consequences of this rigid stance are apparent to battered wives, who can readily attest to the pitfalls of a no-divorce or limited divorce posture.

A more balanced approach regards marriage not only as a social status and legal institution, but also as a *lived moral relation*. Normatively speaking, marriage is "a moral relation involving the binding of two persons, freely and in good faith, in the intention to live together, support each other, and grow in the capacity for caring (not merely caring for each other, but caring) through their mutual lifetime."[46] This definition helps clarify the actions that violate the relationship by harming the individuals involved, including children who may be brought into the marital family. During the course of a couple's history together, there may also be a diminishment of their promised care for each other and for others beyond their twosome. Significantly, this definition also does not limit marriage to heterosexual couplings, nor does it depend on legal authorization.

Philosopher Richard Mohr draws a similar contrast between marriage as legally constituted and as a lived moral reality. Contrary to those who assert that the law (that is, the state) has sole authority to create social relations (on the model of contracts, not covenants), Mohr argues, on the one hand, that marriage does not exist independently of the legal system and the regulatory power of the state. On the other hand, marriage is a relational process that cannot be constituted by law even though it is often "helped or hindered" by law. To grasp the living reality of being married, marriage must be understood as "intimacy given substance in the medium of everyday life, the day-to-day. Marriage is the fused intersection," Mohr offers, "of love's sanctity and necessity's demand."[47]

Both elements, intimacy and the routine demands of everyday life, are required. Some intimate relations, including so-called Great Loves (Cleopatra and Marc Anthony, Catherine and Heathcliff), burn brightly with heat and passion but, lacking the everyday exchanges of "breakfasts and tire-changes," fail to qualify as authentic marriages. Other relationships, such as housemates or college roommates, require tending to the "common necessities of life" and the sharing of ordinary household chores, such as cooking, cleaning, and even finances, but they also lack something essential to marriage: the trust and transparency established through sexual and other intimacies, along with the mutual commitment expressed over time to seek the partner's happiness and well-being.

This kind of relational substance is not, and cannot be, a legal creation even though authentic marriages may well be enhanced by public policy. As Mohr observes, "First and foremost, marriage changes strangers-at-law into next-of-kin with all the rights which this status entails."[48] These rights and privileges make conjoined life easier, but they do not make a marriage happen. Morally speaking, a marriage happens not when the legal status is conferred or even when a wedding ceremony takes place, but only over time through "the sacred valuing of love [that] must come from within and realize itself over time through little sacrifices in day-to-day existence."[49] If marriage is understood as a relational process for deepening moral connection, then many gay men and lesbians already exemplify this reality, even in their extralegal nonmarriages.

The disestablishment of the marital family

The extension of marriage rights to lesbians and gay men will no doubt change prevailing notions of family, but family has never been one fixed thing. Demographers, in documenting the diversity of family patterns in a recent study of North American families, illustrate how family is not a settled category:

Recently, one of us had the opportunity to attend the wedding of a close friend's daughter. As with most weddings, the event came off beautifully, despite the complexity of the seating arrangements required to accommodate all of the bride's and groom's various family members. The bride, age 29, was conceived outside marriage at a time when nonmarital births were less common than today. Her biological parents married shortly before her birth but did not feel financially able to care for her and therefore placed her for adoption. She was adopted as an infant and raised by two adoptive parents, who were present at the wedding.

In her mid-20s, the bride sought out her birth parents and discovered that subsequent to her adoption, they had two other daughters who were now of college age. The bride's two full biological sisters, whom she met as adults, were bridesmaids in the wedding. When the bride sought her birth parents, she found two biological parents no longer married to each other but open to a relationship with the daughter they had long ago placed for adoption. Thus her biological mother and her mother's cohabitating partner attended the wedding. Her biological father, who had subsequently married again, also attended the wedding, along with his second wife and their adopted ten-year-old daughter, who was the flower girl in the wedding.

Indeed, it is difficult to describe all the relatives of the bride who were present to witness her marriage. By some counts, the bride must be said to have had three mothers at her wedding — an adoptive mother, a biological mother, and a stepmother (her biological father's current wife). When she established connections with her biological parents, she also found two biological siblings and another sibling not biologically related to her (the adopted daughter of her biological father).

Needless to say, the groom's relatives had their hands full just trying to figure out how all the bride's guests were related to each other. Yet the groom's family was only somewhat less complicated. The groom's parents were divorced, and the groom's mother attended with her same-sex cohabiting partner. His father also attended the wedding, with his second wife and their thirteen-year-old son, the groom's half brother.[50]

This story may amuse, but it also illustrates the culturally powerful ways in which wedding ceremonies "make families happen," at least for heterosexual couples, and how entrance into married life marks the attainment of adult status. This anecdote also signifies the difficulties, especially during a time of cultural flux, of trying to predict family systems. A newly wed couple may bring into their marriage complex histories and convoluted interpersonal ties that, as this example shows, might well weave together an intricate family web that includes "a nonmarital pregnancy; two adoptions; child rearing by biological parents, stepparents, and adoptive parents; two marital disruptions; remarriages; and both same-sex and heterosexual cohabitation."[51]

Although North American debates are heated when it comes to the marital family and public policy, the heat is due less to disagreements about demographic changes during the last quarter century and more to the ideological character of these disputes and to the conflicting interests the contestants represent. Various parties ascribe widely divergent meanings to family changes and draw radically different implications. Because a divisive "culture war"[52] rages about the future of North American society, it is not surprising that analysts differ greatly in their assessments of what is going on, what has gone wrong, and what must be done to set things right.

To illustrate this conflict, consider the divergent interpretations of two sociologists of the family. David Popenoe, a Rutgers University professor and co-director of the National Marriage Project, argues that the American family is in unprecedented decline. From his perspective, the source of the problem is evident. Traditional marriage is being widely rejected. It no longer commands the respect it deserves as the bedrock institution that guarantees social stability and continuity from one generation to the next. To a great extent, existing families, he contends, no longer provide the care needed for rearing children or for satisfying the emotional and psychological needs of their adult members.

While other social theorists also speak of decline, they do not necessarily locate the crisis (or its cause) *within* the family. Moreover, what
is in decline may not be the family, but rather the overly idealized
(white, suburban) nuclear family and its monopoly on the definition
of what constitutes "real" family. This so-called traditional family pattern, Judith Stacey contends, was never widely applicable to begin
with and certainly not to poor communities or communities of color.
This marital family model is a relatively recent historical creation,
which she argues is "no longer viable, or even desirable" even within
white, affluent communities.

Although Stacey shares Popenoe's concern about the negative consequences of family changes on children, she refrains from locating the
problem as the family itself, nor does she blame changes in cultural attitudes about marriage, women's roles, nonmarital childbirth, or single
parenting. Rather, Stacey locates the problem in a rapidly globalizing
capitalist economy and its disruptive consequences for the marital
family. These disruptions include widening economic disparities between rich and poor (with a diminishing middle class), a precipitous
decline in industrial jobs with decent pay and benefits, and the rising
necessity of income from two or more adult wage earners to (begin to)
secure economic viability for poor families and the consumer lifestyle
of more affluent ones. All these changes have left less time and energy
for active parenting and community involvement, including participation in religious institutions and other voluntary organizations. At
the same time, in contrast to Popenoe, Stacy is willing to "emphasize
the positive aspects of changes in women's opportunities that have
accompanied changes in their roles in the family."[53]

In analyzing the present context, French demographer Louis Rous-
sel suggests that the year 1965 marks an "axis of change" for advanced
industrialized sectors of the globe. A change of historic proportions is
well underway not only in terms of economic arrangements, but also
in marriage and family patterns.[54] In my judgment, this seismic cultural shift is the proper context for situating the current debate over
same-sex marriage. A certain model of family, the marital (or nuclear)
family, so familiar in the post–World War II period, has been culturally

displaced. Because of this disestablishment and the public challenge by the LBGT rights movement to heterosexual marital exclusivism, a sharply contested cultural debate has burst forth about marriage and the state.

While there is no disagreement about marriage and family patterns changing, there is controversy about whether these changes are irrevocable and whether to ignore, resist, or support their advance. Because this marriage and family debate is also about the future of society, two questions lie at the heart of the matter: how should the problem be named, and who has the authority to name it and propose strategies for moving forward?[55] Before analyzing how various parties to the same-sex marriage debate respond, the next chapter considers the benefits of adopting a justice lens for gaining perspective about these concerns.

CHAPTER TWO

A Justice Lens

> *I begin with injustice . . . because*
> *it is the only honest place to begin,*
> *given the realities of our world.*[1]
>
> — KAREN LEBACQZ

FROM A PROGRESSIVE CHRISTIAN PERSPECTIVE, a life well lived is
filled with passion and conviction about seeking justice in all
things. This chapter examines the merits of adopting a justice lens to
analyze the debates on same-sex marriage.

Abundant life for all

By justice making I mean the never-ending project of setting wrongs
right, strengthening connections that are respectful and fair among
individuals and groups, and making communities more inclusive and
welcoming of difference. Seeking justice as rightly related community
lies at the very heart of a liberating spirituality. A passion for justice also requires assuming certain responsibilities: to notice things,
name them by their right name, weigh their moral significance, and
then devise action-steps to keep things as they are or change them,
depending on what, to the best of our knowledge, will enhance life together. From a religious perspective, justice making is the most fitting
response to the Spirit's invitation to share life on this planet so that
both humans and nonhumans, as well as the earth itself, may flourish.
Simply put, justice is the virtue of seeking abundant life for all.[2]

Advocacy for justice is a risky, sometimes perilous enterprise, especially given the entrenchment of moral evil in the human heart
and psyche, as well as in social institutions and everyday customs and

36

conventions. These days justice making is particularly fraught with difficulties because this is a time of cultural crisis. The term "crisis" refers to more than a period of accelerated change. As used here, it refers to a protracted, fast-paced, and highly conflicted process of global restructuring that is disrupting social (and planetary) relations at every level. The primary engine of this world-altering change is economic. Transnational corporations and entities such as the World Trade Organization, International Monetary Fund, and World Bank are seeking to further integrate the world's nation-states into a single capitalist market economy.[3] This globalization process, long underway but now gaining momentum everywhere, is changing not only political and economic macrosystems, but also the very contours of personal and family life. It is not far-fetched to speak of a crisis in sexuality and family as one component of a larger, systemic shift being propelled by globalization.[4]

Living during tempestuous times is challenging. Everywhere the rules of the game are being rewritten, but few people are ever consulted in the process. Almost everything familiar is changing, from jobs to welfare policies, from banking practices to international relations, from education to mass-market entertainment, from Internet communication to family and gender politics. As Nobel poet laureate Octavio Paz cautions, this is more than a time of change; it is also a "change of times."[5] During such a moment, it may be wise to pay attention once more to "the old moralist's claim that understanding itself is a moral act." When everything seems to be going on at once, what we *choose* to notice discloses much about our values and commitments.[6] This mandate to attend to things that matter has weighed heavily on me ever since I made the decision to write a book about same-sex marriage. Given everything going on, I've had to ask myself repeatedly, how important *is* this issue? Isn't marriage a tired old topic, and furthermore, what does marriage — same-sex or otherwise — have to do with justice?

Justice in intimate places

Throughout this study, I make a wager that same-sex marriage is far from inconsequential. In fact, I find that this debate both reflects and contributes to broader social debates about moral values, personal commitments, public policy, and the direction and pace of cultural change. In church and society, the topics of marriage, sexuality, gender, and homosexuality have become flashpoints of contentiousness as people struggle, inside themselves and with others, to clarify normative expectations for family and social life. No matter the opinions people hold, disagreements only intensify whenever the modifier "same-sex" is added.

In sorting out how proponents and opponents view same-sex marriage, I, too, have an agenda. My interest is threefold: first, to draw on feminist and queer/gay liberation moral wisdom to critique oppressive religious and social understandings of marriage and family; second, to explore how various parties link (or fail to link) love and intimacy with justice; and third, to develop a compelling case for *ethical* marriage as an honorable, though not exclusive, place in which LBGT and non-LBGT people can live responsibly as sexual persons. As a Christian ethicist and gay man, I contend that justice and love are always matters of public — that is, communal — importance. My conviction is that one way to strengthen the common good is by strengthening people's capacities for entering into and sustaining good partnerships and vibrant families. Good marriages reflect an ongoing commitment to living justly — rightly, respectfully, compassionately — in intimate as well as other social relations.

That said, the fact of the matter is that marriage, family, and sexuality have not customarily been linked with justice. It behooves us to ask, therefore, why has there been an absence of justice discourse about intimate matters? The reasons are complex. For one thing, justice has been associated with men's public "world-building" engagements, not with the so-called private realm of women and children. As long as men are the primary authors of treatises on justice, androcentrism will regard marriage and family as inconsequential matters compared to empire- and cathedral-building. Because of the pervasiveness of this masculinist bias, feminist theorist Susan Moller Okin has observed, "It is not easy to think about marriage and the family in terms of justice" because "we do not readily associate justice with intimacy."[7]

Second, because marriage and family have been, to a great extent, idealized and romanticized within North American white Protestantism, little attention has been given to harsher realities, including sexual exploitation, abuse of power, and oppression among intimates. During recent decades, feminist scholars and activists, including religious feminists, have had to struggle on a variety of fronts to "change the subject,"[8] both in terms of who is authorized to speak (and who is recognized as speaking with authority) and in terms of the topics considered worthwhile. Women and gay men of all colors, because they have been judged deficient and morally suspect due to their association with the body, sexuality, and so-called private or intimate matters, have good reason to recognize that "in the real world, justice is a virtue of fundamental importance for families as it is for other social institutions."[9]

Distributive justice is most often associated with allocating goods and resources equitably, including tangible goods such as food, shelter, and health care. However, justice should also be concerned with intangible goods, such as attention, respect, and care. Furthermore, a justice-focused discourse about marriage requires dealing with imbalances of power and vulnerability between intimates and with the social structures and norms that reinforce these inequalities. For better or worse, power and, therefore, injustices shape every aspect of life, including intimacy and eroticism. However, without an ethical framework that explicitly opens up these matters for critical reflection, people may not notice or respond when injustices arise "close to the skin" and, literally, at home.

To be adequate, a justice framework must assess the microdynamics between intimates, but also the larger macrostructures that bear on intimate life, including racism, sexism, heterosexism, and economic inequities. Above all, a justice ethic must address the use and misuse of power. Because intimate relations are also power relations set within larger social structures, people concerned with justice (and its essential companion, compassion) must come to greater awareness about how marriage and family are arenas in which injustice occurs. Struggles for survival and self-respect are often intense between intimates, precisely because male (and heterosexual) power and privilege are so firmly entrenched and taken for granted as the way things should be. For these reasons, there is nothing easy about confronting injustice within marriage or family life, nor any guarantee that even intimates who genuinely love each other will do right or make justice real between them. As survivors of abuse can testify, injustice between intimates creates no fewer casualties than injustices "out there." So-called private or "merely" personal injuries and insults are often accompanied, as well, by betrayal and trauma that are made all the more painful because of the cultural expectation that family is where "love happens" and where people should expect to find nurture and care, not abuse or exploitation.

Justice bears on marriage and family life in yet another way because of the education of children and their moral formation as citizens. The family has long been regarded as the primary developmental context for forming human identity and deepening sociability. "If justice cannot at least begin to be learned from our day-to-day experience within the family," Okin writes, "it seems futile to expect that it can be developed anywhere else. Without just families, how can we expect to have a just society?"[10] I would ask, additionally, how can we expect to have a just society without *ethical* and *just marriages*, that is, marriages that exhibit a deep regard for mutual respect, caring, and a fair sharing of power, as well as an equitable distribution of the joys, burdens, and responsibilities of life together?

The prospect of same-sex marriage raises normative ethical questions about justice between intimates, about the very purposes and forms of marriage and other intimate relations in contemporary society, and about society's (and the churches') obligations toward couples who seek to enter into long-term commitments. As discussed in the previous chapter, such debates are not new. The history of U.S. family law and public policy is replete with similar struggles and acrimonious debates about women's legal status to own property, their right to divorce and not lose custody of their minor children, and their legal recourse to marital rape. Interestingly, each of these concerns gained prominence also during times of social and economic upheaval. Marriage troubles, it seems, are often a sign of a more extensive cultural crisis.

The bigger picture

Efforts to alter cultural practices, as well as public policy, regarding marriage and family life must take two factors into account: the capacity of humans to shape the future through their collective moral agency and the social nexus in which they must act. That context includes the institutional structures and cultural ideologies that govern human sexuality, marriage, and family and make them appear natural and unchangeable. Therefore, both the personal and political, the economic and sociocultural must be considered if we are to discern what is going on. Two macro-level developments bear especially on marriage and family: on the one hand, globalization and the massive dislocations and suffering it has generated and, on the other hand, the emergence of grassroots social justice movements to redress that suffering, revitalize community, and protect the earth.

The globalization of market capitalism has disrupted social, economic, and family patterns in the United States and elsewhere due to rapid deindustrialization and the subsequent rise of a managerial service economy. Technological changes and the massive relocation of manufacturing jobs to low-wage sectors inside and outside the United States have created a surplus labor pool and a dramatic increase in part-time, low-wage jobs with little job security and minimal if any benefits. Because these jobs do not generate a living wage that can support a household with a wife at home with dependent children, families have come to depend on at least two adult wager-earners for some measure of economic stability. Heightened consumerism and personal indebtedness make matters even more tenuous for many families. Such structural changes are producing enormous stresses and giving rise to fear, uncertainty, and in some quarters, a quest to identify a "designated enemy" that can be faulted for these troubles.

Economic pressures, in conjunction with women's rising expectations of enhanced participation in economic, political, and cultural life, have led to increasing numbers of women working outside the home during and beyond their childrearing years. Women's entry as wageworkers has come at a time when the cost of raising children is increasing and finding quality childcare has become more difficult. Many heterosexual couples respond to such pressures by reducing family size. Faced with inadequate social and economic supports, women struggle with the stresses and strains of constantly having to invent personal solutions for juggling responsibilities in the workforce along with a "second shift" at home. In addition, worker mobility has further disrupted extended family and community connections. All these changes have affected conventional gender roles and expectations, especially for white, middle-class women. Once settled convictions about love, sex, marriage, and family are now being vigorously reexamined throughout the globe.

The other macro-level development that bears powerfully on marriage, gender relations, family, and sexuality is the emergence of grassroots feminist, womanist, mujerista, and LBGT liberation movements in the United States and elsewhere. Each offers sustained critiques of racism, sexism, heterosexism, economic inequities, ecological degradation, and other forms of oppression. These diverse social justice movements are promoting a politics of cultural transformation. Through education and democratic community building, they seek to alter unjust social policies, realign institutional power dynamics, and critique cultural norms that devalue some identities while overvaluing others.

Initially, a particular group or movement may organize in response to a single perceived injustice or what appears as a discrete problem, such as securing women's legal right to reproductive self-determination or gaining the full participation of people with disabilities in political, economic, and cultural life. However, progressives have learned several key lessons over years of struggle: first, the wisdom of employing an interstructural analysis of social oppressions ("none is free until all are free"), and, second, the desirability of building broad, expansive coalitions. Only an inclusive, multicultural movement that organizes across broadly intersecting lines of social difference will ever be positioned to make real-life connections among various oppressions, incorporate an economic structural analysis, focus on both personal and institution transformation, and develop change strategies with a commitment not to demonize or scapegoat others.

In considering a broadly multicultural "politics of inclusion," social activist Suzanne Pharr speaks of the need for a comprehensive moral vision: "We can no longer afford single-issue politics that look at the small picture and miss the big one."[11] The emphasis on linkages — connecting issues and people — is certainly done for pragmatic, strategic reasons, but also as a matter of moral conviction. Across socially defined differences, people share a common humanity and common destiny. The great social lie is to claim that some groups are superior, others inferior.

A politics of recognition makes same-sex marriage thinkable

Throughout most of the twentieth century, homosexuality has been considered a crime, mental illness, and/or sin. Legally, gay men and lesbians have been regarded as potential felons, subject to criminal prosecution by the state for sexual activity between consenting adults. Culturally, they have been outcasts, vulnerable to ostracism, job loss, and rejection by family, church, and community whenever their identity was made public. Religiously speaking, homosexuality has been the love that dared not speak — or pray — its name. For these reasons, until very recently state and religious recognition of same-sex marriage was unthinkable.

What has dramatically changed the cultural climate is the emergence of a LBGT rights/liberation movement. This broad-based social justice movement marks the 1969 Stonewall rebellion as its beginning point, when gay men and cross-dressers, many of them poor and Hispanic, fought back against police harassment at an underground bar in New York's Greenwich Village. Earlier, during the 1950s Cold War era, homophile groups had bravely challenged the status quo and pressed for the elimination of anti-sodomy laws, a major source of state persecution. Invoking a right to privacy, these early reformers had insisted that the state should be neutral toward homosexuality and not interfere with consensual sex between (same-sex) adults. In essence, a sexual minority was arguing to be "left alone" by the cultural majority.

Legal scholar William Eskridge proposes the term "politics of protection" to describe these early efforts to protect private spaces from state intrusion and to safeguard such gay institutions as bars, clubs, and journals. "Under such a regime," Eskridge observes, "same-sex marriage was not a realistic goal."[12]

With the rise of a gay rights/liberation movement in the late 1960s and the increased visibility of LBGT people in families, neighborhoods, and other social institutions, a shift has taken place from a politics of (self-)protection toward an LBGT politics of recognition. Eradication of sodomy laws has been a necessary first step toward gay emancipation. In the early 1970s, all but one state had anti-sodomy laws;[13] as late as 2003, these laws remained on the books in fifteen states.[14] Once decriminalization of consensual, adult same-sex sexual activity takes place, efforts to enact anti-discrimination legislation follows. Many states and municipalities have passed laws and ordinances making it illegal to deny jobs, housing, credit, and public accommodation on the basis of sexual orientation.

A politics of recognition seeks more than noninterference from the state or toleration by the wider community, even though both are significant gains. LBGT people are seeking respect as well as recognition as equal citizens. At a minimum, the state should provide the same protections and benefits to gay people as it does to other citizens, including recognition of their primary intimate relationships and families. During the last quarter of the twentieth century, a gay-centered, gay-affirmative politics of recognition has radically transformed the cultural sensibilities and life expectations of LBGT people. In the early 1970s, the American Psychiatric Association removed homosexuality from its list of mental disorders. Religious groups began a process of intense study and internal debate that led many to reevaluate human sexuality and remove longstanding barriers that prevent LBGT people from participating fully in the life and leadership of their religious communities. An explicitly gay-affirming, gay-led denomination was formed in the late 1960s, the Universal Fellowship of Metropolitan Community Churches, and this fledgling church early on began to offer blessings for same-sex couples as they entered into holy unions.

During the early 1970s, a handful of same-sex couples sought to acquire marriage licenses. Couples in Minnesota, Washington state, and Kentucky filed lawsuits when their requests were denied. During this same period, a sympathetic city clerk in Boulder, Colorado, managed to issue marriage licenses to at least six lesbian and gay couples before the state attorney general's office intervened and put a stop to the illicit activity. Although none of those couples was successful in gaining legal recognition of their unions, there were other kinds of gains. Because of this civil disobedience, as one social commentator has written, there were "news accounts depicting gay people in a positive manner and informing many heterosexual and gay people for the first time that some gay people were demanding that their relationships be recognized."[15]

Backlash from the Right

The strength and moderate success of this gay-positive social justice movement has precipitated opposition from social and religious conservatives espousing "traditional family values" and strenuously objecting to "normalizing" homosexuality.[16] Two events in the 1980s demonstrated the power of this backlash. First, the Sharon Kowalski case highlighted the legal vulnerability of same-sex couples because they lack the basic rights and protections that the state automatically confers to married couples, including the right of one spouse to make medical decisions for the other. In this instance, the legal system supported the parents of Sharon Kowalski, a young woman who had suffered an accident and was hospitalized in a persistent vegetative state. During a seven-year legal battle, the courts denied her lesbian life partner, Karen Thompson, access to Sharon or authority to make decisions regarding Sharon's health and ongoing care even though the two women had exchanged rings and purchased a home together.[17]

A second setback for the gay rights movement was the 1986 U.S. Supreme Court decision in *Bowers v. Hardwick* denying constitutional protection of same-sex sexual activity. While the Court acknowledged that a right of privacy safeguards marriage and family intimacy, its conventional picture of family placed gay men and lesbians outside the circle of protected intimacy. For gays and lesbians to claim a right to state protection of their intimate partnerships and families was, in the Court's judgment, nothing less than "facetious."[18]

Despite such setbacks and a major anti-gay campaign by the Christian Right, the LBGT community has continued to press for full rights of citizenship, including the right to civil marriage. For marriage traditionalists, the unthinkable happened in 1993. The Hawaii Supreme Court ruled in *Baehr v. Lewin* (later *Baehr v. Miike*) that denial of marriage to same-sex couples was a form of sex discrimination. Nina Baehr, a lesbian woman, had gone to court because she had been denied the right to marry because her partner happened to be a woman rather than a man. In responding to the case, the Court ruled that because of Hawaii's constitutional guarantee against sex discrimination, the burden was placed on the state to justify its prohibition as appropriate and necessary. The state offered several arguments, but its main contention was that marriage is an institution designed for childrearing, that the best interest of children is to be raised by mixed-gender parents, and that parents of only one sex could not provide adequate gender modeling. None of these claims proved persuasive. "Not only did the court hold that the state failed to prove its assertions," legal scholar Yuval Merin has written. "It also stated that if same-sex marriage were allowed, the children being raised by lesbian or gay parents and same-sex couples *might benefit* because they might obtain certain protections and benefits that come with or become available as a result of marriage."[19] However, the Hawaii Supreme Court never gave its final ruling because the Hawaii electorate, in the meantime, passed a constitutional amendment allowing the state legislature to restrict marriage to heterosexual unions.

Momentum toward state recognition of same-sex marriage again picked up speed in the late 1990s when three Vermont couples, Stan Baker and Peter Harrigan, Nina Beck and Stacy Jolles, and Lois Farnham and Holly Puterbaugh, sued for the right to be issued marriage licenses. As discussed in chapter 1, in a landmark 1999 decision, the Vermont State Supreme Court ruled that same-sex couples are, indeed, entitled to the very same protections and benefits that the law provides for mixed-gender married couples. However, the Court sidestepped the issue of whether same-sex couples should be granted marriage licenses or be allowed to marry legally. Instead, it focused on equal access to equivalent rights and benefits. The state legislature was instructed to devise a mechanism for establishing such access for same-sex couples, and it created a new legal option, civil union, to meet the Court's mandate.

If these judicial and legislative victories were not enough to upset marriage traditionalists, a sea change has also been taking place in U.S. society in terms of gender, marriage, and family.[20] Two social scientists, in introducing their study of recent family changes, remark that while it is unlikely that marriage will disappear, it is not far-fetched to say that "heterosexual marriage will lose its privileged place among other forms of couples."[21] Nothing chills a marriage traditionalist more than the prospect of a decline in status for heterosexual marriage, except perhaps something else these social theorists also observe: "Perhaps the most striking change during the last thirty years is not so much the very real increase in extramarital sexual activity, out-of-wedlock births, divorce, and serial marriages but *the way our society has accommodated such previously condemned practices.*"[22]

Adopting a justice lens

It is within this highly polarized social context that the debate about same-sex marriage has unfolded. Contextualizing marriage alerts us to how political and ideological dynamics play out now as background, now as foreground: globalization's disruptive impact on families and communities, the emergence of grassroots justice movements for gender, racial, and sexual justice, and a well-financed and organized backlash from the Right. In making sense of these dynamics, the choice of interpretive lens is crucial.

To grasp the meaning of *sexual* justice, we should first clarify what justice means. In *Justice in an Unjust World*, Christian ethicist Karen Lebacqz acknowledges that justice is an elusive concept. Not everyone who cries out for justice — or against injustice — necessarily means the same thing. While there is no single, objective, and universally agreed upon standard, Lebacqz recommends adopting a historical, experiential approach that takes as its starting point the lived experience of injustice in its multiple dimensions: as political disenfranchisement, economic disadvantage, and cultural marginality.[23]

In order to pursue justice, it is also necessary to *have a feel for* actual experiences of injustice, of the pain and suffering incurred not only because of individual acts of meanness and cruelty, but also as a consequence of status quo power arrangements that grant privileges to some at the expense of others. Gaining a cognitive and affective appreciation of injustice as lived reality requires, first and foremost, listening to the pain-filled stories of those who have experienced an injustice. Second, we must rely on the social sciences to demonstrate how structural dynamics of power and oppression have perpetuated that pain. For this reason, what churns at the heart of every justice struggle is conflict over how to interpret the world and whose authority counts in that naming.

In order to gain a truthful rendering of what's going on, more is needed than facts and information. A shift in interpretive framework is called for, so that preference is no longer given reflexively to the conventional wisdom of the day. Instead, alternative truths from the margins must be seriously entertained as sources of moral insight.[24] Therefore, adopting a justice lens involves intentionally viewing the world from the perspective of those who are made to suffer and are now rising up, as best they can, to resist their oppression.

Accordingly, engaging in an open-ended process of doing justice requires, first of all, solidarity — a real standing with and for the oppressed.[25] Second, justice making requires a different epistemological stance. A more truthful, accurate rendering of reality is possible only by listening to and learning from those who have been harmed and yet resist their lack of power and status as fully human. Although the rapist, too, has a story to tell and should be listened to with care and even respect for his personhood, the one raped occupies the more privileged position of naming the true character of their encounter.

Setting things right will require attending to both parties, but doing justice — correcting the injustice and possibly restoring the ruptured relationship — also requires partisanship, the taking of sides in order to do justice to both parties, the victim and the victimizer, as well as the community.

From a progressive Christian perspective, justice involves more than formal equality (treating like cases alike) or fair distribution (giving each person his or her due), important as both notions are for community life. Rather, justice is best grasped as an ongoing process of active intervention to correct injustices by reordering skewed power dynamics. The intended goal is to empower disenfranchised persons and groups so that they may live as respected, participatory members of the community, empowered to pursue their own life projects.

Catholic moral theologian Daniel Maguire agrees that justice seeks to "put an end to marginality."[26] Doing justice means working not just for the *inclusion* of some, but for the *transformation* of community itself so that all may participate meaningfully and share enough resources to thrive. In drawing on Christian insights, Maguire states: "The Bible does two things: it identifies justice with God, which is the highest compliment available . . . , and it predicts total social and political collapse if this kind of justice is not realized."[27] Moreover, injustice takes shape primarily as exclusion, deprivation, and exploitation. Since social and economic inequalities build up over time, *social* imbalance requires *social* redress. As Maguire explains, "A group which has been disadvantaged as a group needs reinstatement into the sharing patterns in which essential goods are distributed in a society."[28]

Justice as redistribution and recognition

Redistribution is one component of social justice, but it does not fulfill all that justice requires. Justice is also about recognition of persons *as persons*. Based on indebtedness or owingness, justice is grounded in the perception that others, too, are persons of worth. As part of the community, they have a right to make claims on others. As Maguire writes,

"We show what we think persons are worth by what we ultimately concede is due to them." This insight leads to a jarring conclusion: "If we deny persons justice, we have declared them worthless!"[29]

These reflections by Christian theologians resonate with the insights of feminist and critical social theorists, especially that justice consists of redistribution and recognition. Each aspect must be addressed insofar as injustice is experienced, on the one hand, as economic disadvantage and exploitation and, on the other hand, as cultural disrespect and marginalization. Both socioeconomic injustice and cultural injustice are pervasive in society. While often intertwined, each requires a different form of redress. As Nancy Fraser suggests, "the remedy for economic injustice is political and economic restructuring of some sort." In contrast, the remedy for cultural injustice is "some sort of cultural or symbolic change" that would result in recognition of the group in question.[30]

While cultural injustice often takes the form of stereotyping a group (women, people of color, gays and lesbians), it may also render a group invisible, without social standing, and, above all, without the power and authority to define reality on its own terms, including its own identity and culture. For lesbians and gay men, as well as bisexual and transgender people, being culturally oppressed means being defined by others and rendered the Other, serving as object for ridicule and pity but not recognized and valued as co-equal subject.

Gay oppression takes the form of cultural displacement. Injustice happens less from efforts to keep gay people "in their place," a strategy reflective of the repression and suppression of women and people of color, and more from having no place in which gayness is visible and represented as a valid way of being human. Specifically, gays are denied the right — and the very possibility — of loving humanly.[31] Because sexual oppression affects non-gay as well as gay people (although dissimilarly), the correction of injustice requires, as Fraser contends, "the wholesale transformation of societal patterns of representation, interpretation, and communication in ways that would change *everybody's* sense of self."[32]

Gay oppression is primarily a matter of cultural disrespect and enforced invisibility. Homosexuality is demarcated a "despised sexuality." Same-sex relationships are not seen as examples of, much less as models for, loving, intimate bonding between persons. This marginality is accompanied by and results in economic disempowerment. The denial of the civil right to marry has bread-and-butter consequences for same-sex couples. In being denied access to the goods and privileges extended to married couples as a matter of entitlement, gay couples lose out on everything from inheritance rights to eligibility for heath and life insurance that covers marital spouses.

For the LBGT community, group pride becomes a powerful and empowering corrective to negative stereotyping. "Coming out" is intentionally deployed as a political strategy to counter the invisibility imposed on gay people as "unreal," deviant, and not truly human. The goal is not to reverse the tables by imposing a "gay chauvinism" that idealizes queerness as the exclusively valid human identity. For one thing, the LBGT community lacks the power to impose a "queer norm." More important, the LBGT movement seeks to *end* oppression, not impose it on others. Moreover, justice depends not on eliminating social difference, but rather on reordering difference so that it is no longer construed in terms of superiority and inferiority. The justice goal is difference without domination.

Heterosexism, the institutionalizing of heterosexuality as the exclusively normative way to be human, is constructed on the basis of devaluing sexual difference. It involves the universalizing of heterosexual experience and cultural norms from a supposedly neutral, but in fact privileged position of power, and "normalcy," the measuring of those who are different as deviant ("failed" heterosexuals) and inferior (sinful, criminal, mentally ill). Resistance to heterosexist oppression requires, on the part of the culturally defined Other, a subversive move to become self-defining. Seen in this light, such cultural events as Gay Pride parades are public demonstrations for asserting cultural identity and mounting political resistance. Within the LBGT community "getting married" is also viewed, at least by some, as a *political* act, not merely as the making of a personal commitment between two "private selves." It is assumed that heterosexual couples are also "doing politics" and pursuing a political agenda when they marry. Marriage is a valuable means for claiming *public* space, *public* recognition, and a *public* identity.

Correcting injustice

The work of doing sexual justice involves critiquing an entire universe of cultural assumptions and everyday practices about the "right way" of doing sex, gender roles, desire, and intimacy. It also requires bringing to critical consciousness a vast array of taken-for-granted assumptions that most people simply go along with, often unconsciously, without ever noticing their coercive and harmful effects.

Not all oppression is, of course, conscious or the result of intentional acts of oppressiveness, even though it is true that violence directed at gay people is pervasive and gay bashing is a common "sport," especially among young males.[33] As Iris Marion Young observes: "Oppression in this sense is [better understood as] structural, rather than the result of a few people's choices or policies. Its causes are embedded in unquestioned norms, habits, and symbols, in the assumptions underlying institutional rules and the collective consequences of following those rules." Accordingly, "Oppression designates the disadvantage and injustice some people suffer not because a tyrannical power coerces them, but because of the everyday practices of a well-intentioned liberal society."[34] Although there are, indeed, individuals who do mean and violent acts to LBGT people, the structural character of oppression means "an oppressed group need not have a correlate oppressing group."

Oppression may be unconscious and unintended. At the same time, for every oppressed group there is a privileged or overadvantaged group.[35] Those with social privilege, including people who are white-skinned, affluent, male, heterosexual, able-bodied, and combinations of these and other social markers, typically think of themselves as occupying the center or, as educator Peggy McIntosh writes, "as morally neutral, normative, and average, and also ideal, so that when we work to benefit others, this is seen as work which will allow 'them' to be more like 'us.' "[36] Those with social power and privilege think of themselves as "real." They have the luxury of thinking of their lives individualistically rather than politically because they are not burdened by oppression and injustice. However, living "at the center" means having "power over" others and the cultural permission *not to see* the non-normative "Other" as someone also real.[37]

If injustice is systemic and embedded in cultural norms and practices that shape everyday life, then "simply" disapproving of those structures will not change them. Individual acts of kindness and generosity may ameliorate the consequences of oppression, but they too are insufficient. A systems shift and a transformation of cultural values are necessary.

If justice is an ongoing process of correcting injustices, then it may be helpful to consider three aspects of sexual injustice and begin identifying what is required to set things right.[38]

First, sex-negativity is pervasive in Western culture, largely influenced by patriarchal Christianity's discomfort with body, women, and nature.

Second, heterosexuality has been institutionalized as the definitive measure by which all other sexualities are judged. Normative heterosexuality is also compulsory, demanded of all persons male and female, regardless of sexual interest and identity (including asexuality), backed up by violence, and "normalized" by stigmatizing and making invisible other erotic patterns, especially homoeroticism.

Third, sexual injustice is marked not only by the enforcement of compulsory heterosexuality, but also by abuse, exploitation, and other forms of violence.

Normative heterosexuality as culturally scripted requires male dominance and female subordination. The norm of male-dominant heterosexuality organizes social and sexual exchange around men's needs and especially men's pleasure. For this reason, many heterosexual women report little or no satisfaction from their interactions with their male partners, including their intimate erotic interactions.

Injustice as wrong relation has become eroticized, such that *unequal* power or domination has become a "turn on" for many men (and some women, as well) who are socialized into accepting that "being manly" means gaining access to and control over women as conquests. Patriarchal marriage, the intimate yet hierarchical bonding of two social *un*equals, portrays "good sex" as nonmutual exchange. Although idealized and defended by church and state, patriarchal marriage is unethical. Its cultural hegemony is a moral scandal.

In light of these dynamics, sexual justice would include the following:

First, in the face of pervasive sex-negativity, sexual justice requires honoring the goodness of human bodies and of sexuality as a remarkable *spiritual* power to express care and respect through bodily touching and deep communication.

Second, in the face of compulsory heterosexuality, sexual justice requires recognition of and respect for sexual difference, including diversities of body shape and size, sexual orientation, and marriage and family patterns.

Third, in the face of sexual violence, abuse, and exploitation, sexual justice calls for respect and care between persons and among groups, as well as the eroticizing of mutuality as the normative expectation between intimate partners. Justice also requires a fair distribution of power and social goods, the enhancement of safety, health, and freedom, especially for the vulnerable, and empowerment so that each and all can participate in shaping social arrangements and cultural expectations.

Two other dimensions of sexual justice are worth noting. As a fourth component, sexual justice involves both claiming rights and assuming responsibilities. This aspect is sometimes underplayed in the same-sex marriage debate, insofar as the focus has been on acquiring the *right to marry* on the part of same-sex couples. However, as we shall see later on, this debate is as much about *responsibility* as it is about civil rights. One way queers are, in fact, dehumanized is by denying them the human capacity for, and interest in, fulfilling basic moral obligations and showing "common decency." Therefore, gay men are caricatured as irresponsible "perpetual teens" acting out uncontrollable sexual urges without regard for "mature" relationships of commitment and durability, especially when sacrifice is called for. Women-who-love-women are dismissed as man-haters and, if they are mothers, as deficient and even dangerous parents.

A fifth and final aspect of sexual justice is solidarity, expressed as concrete answerability to oppressed people. Heterosexual allies have an important role to play in helping to create inclusive, diverse communities that welcome and show genuine respect for LBGT persons. Part of that role is showing a willingness to listen to and learn from the marginalized. It also requires a willingness to *politicize* sexual oppression as a matter of injustice and become engaged in a politics of transformation, aimed not merely to include gay people in social institutions, but to alter norms and structures as necessary, so that all people may be recognized and honored in their full humanity.

Legal scholar Martha Minow speaks about the central concerns of politics as determining "who's in or out, and who gets what."[39] Even how we define family — or, in this instance, marriage — indicates, she continues, "social and political choices about distributing privileges." As we shall see in the next chapter, marriage traditionalists are centrally concerned with these questions, not because they raise the justice question in behalf of LBGT people, but rather because of their determination to preserve marriage as an exclusively heterosexual institution.

CHAPTER THREE

Marriage Traditionalists

> *If ever there was a place*
> *to draw a line, this is it.*[1]
> — STANLEY N. KURTZ

A MONG OPPONENTS of same-sex marriage, Robert H. Knight, director of cultural studies at the Family Research Council, is particularly outspoken. "The law doesn't discriminate against homosexuals," he writes. Rather, "it merely says that each sex must be represented in marriage. Same-sex couples do not qualify. It might be called a partnership, but if it's called marriage, it's a counterfeit version. And counterfeit versions drive out the real thing."[2]

This chapter examines the arguments put forward by opponents of same-sex marriage who identify themselves as marriage traditionalists. (Chapter 5 deals with opponents who define themselves as marriage critics.) Knight is far from alone in his insistence that marriage is, and must remain, an exclusively heterosexual institution. After considering their arguments, the chapter concludes with an assessment of the Right's "politics of preservation," in which maintaining the marital family as a natural hierarchy becomes the centerpiece of a larger social project to uphold and legitimate other inequalities of rank and power.[3]

Definitional objections

Marriage traditionalists insist that marriage is a heterosexual institution and, therefore, necessarily closed to gay men and lesbians. According to both standard definitions and customary usage, the term marriage refers to a union between a man and a woman. As Robert

Knight writes, "When the meaning of a word becomes more inclusive, the exclusivity that it previously defined is lost."[4] Much is at stake, he suggests. "Destroying definitions does enormous damage not only to marriage but to the idea of truth. Calling two lesbians a 'marriage' is telling a lie, and official recognition of this lie breeds the sort of cynicism found in totalitarian societies, where lies are common currency."[5]

The heterosexuality of marriage is grounded in the procreative imperative. Regarded as the favored environment in which to produce and raise children, marriage is also important because it socializes men and women into their properly gendered roles as husbands-fathers and wives-mothers. For traditionalists, because marriage forms persons into responsible "marital citizens," it is indispensable to a thriving society. As Knight explains,

> Marriage . . . brings the two sexes together in a unique legal, social, economic, and spiritual union. . . . No other relationship provides society what marriage does. No other relationship transforms young men and young women into more productive, less selfish, and more mature husbands and wives, and fathers and mothers, than marriage. No other relationship affords children the best economic, emotional and psychological environment. Only as we have drifted from the defense of marriage have we experienced soaring social problems, such as divorce, illegitimacy, sexually-transmitted diseases, and crime. The answer is not to push the envelope further but to restore the primacy of marriage within the law and culture.[6]

As the major "foundational building block for a secure and stable nation," marriage deserves, first of all, special protection by the law. Moreover, because it is also "the heart of family life" and "the key organizing principle behind all civilization," it merits an equally elevated cultural status. On this score, marriage traditionalists are adamant: marriage is "a priority worth encouraging above other kinds of relationships."[7] It ought to be privileged by law, religion, and custom and protected from those who would politicize it with their narrow "gay agenda."

Knight's negative view of homosexuality gives him only additional reason for drawing a restrictive circle around marriage in order to preserve it as an exclusively heterosexual institution. "Societies must have intact families to survive," Knight argues, but "societies do not need any homosexual relationships in order to flourish. To equate them is to lie about them."[8] Moreover, because "marriage reflects the natural moral and social law which is in evidence all over the world," he contends that any radical departure from traditional marriage, including endorsing single-parent families or same-sex marriage, will have serious negative consequences. "No society has loosened sexual morality outside of man-woman marriage," Knight warns, "and survived."[9]

Marriage as heterosexual

Knight's objections to enlarging the marriage paradigm are similar to the concerns cited by other critics of same-sex marriage. In arguing against changes in marriage policy that would include lesbians and gay men, opponents are often pushed to offer more than a definitional argument against same-sex marriage. When pressed, they quickly identify things *about marriage* that they contend make it necessary and proper to limit marriage to heterosexual couples alone.

John Finnis, a New Natural Law scholar, writes that gay men and lesbians are incapable of actualizing the goods of marriage because of who and what they are. His argument runs as follows. The twin purposes of marriage, the procreative and the unitive, are inextricably linked. For a marriage to be authentic *as a marriage*, it requires children (or at least the procreative possibility) and what Finnis calls "real mutuality." Gay male and lesbian couples fail on both scores. First, gays do not procreate. Their unions do not produce the good of children. Second, even though two men or two women may experience some resemblance of mutuality, they cannot achieve the mutuality that Finnis posits is possible only within heterosexual, procreative marriage. To be complete, a relationship must bring together two differently gen-dered persons who truly complement each other in body, psyche, and role. Two men or two women reflect sameness in their connectedness, not difference upon which "real" complementarity depends.

A union also requires heterosexual sex in order to be real marriage. As Finnis explains, genital sexual intercourse between marital spouses "enables them to actualize and experience (and in that sense express) their marriage itself, as a single reality with two blessings (children and mutual affection)."[10] Citing ancient Christian and Stoic philoso-phers, Finnis argues that sex is "decent and acceptable only within marriage." Marital sex is natural and reasonable; nonmarital sex, in-cluding homosexual sexual activity, is neither natural nor reasonable. In fact, Finnis speaks of gay sex as emphatically immoral and "mani-festly unworthy of the human being."[11] For heterosexual couples "the union of the reproductive organs of husband and wife really unites them biologically." The two become "one flesh." For gay people, on the other hand, sex does "no more than provide each partner with an individual gratification," which Finnis believes amounts to noth-ing more than "solitary masturbation."[12] As if to leave no doubt in the reader's mind about which sexual acts are moral, Finnis discretely clarifies in a footnote that "the human mouth is not a reproductive organ,"[13] and by this logic, neither is the anus. Good, morally accept-able sex is penis-in-vagina sex with the capacity for and openness to bringing children into the world.

In Finnis's judgment, same-sex marriage is an oxymoron. Such unions are not capable of achieving the twin goods of marriage, which are producing children and expressing male-female gender comple-mentarity. He contends, further, that gay sexual unions exist for one purpose only, sexual gratification. That purpose is morally suspect. Sexually active gay men and lesbians use the human body instrumen-tally, he writes, in order to experience physical pleasure, a purpose he describes as "morally worthless."[14] Hedonistic pursuit of pleasure lacks a morally significant purpose and, therefore, should be avoided, as should all forms of vice and illicit behavior. Finnis concludes that the state should actively discourage homosexual conduct, even between consenting adults, because the community should never endorse immorality or give it legal sanction. Simply put, same-sex coupling is not the moral equivalent of marriage, but its very antithesis. To support same-sex marriage is to threaten the very meaning of real marriage.

Protestant Christian Max L. Stackhouse also argues against extending the right to marry to same-sex couples. Along with Finnis, he contends that heterosexual marriage is the basic normative structure for human sexuality, attested to by biblical tradition but also "given in creation" as "part of the moral fabric established in the deepest structures of human life."[15] He, too, contends that the "one flesh" union of two people is possible only in heterosexual couplings. As Stackhouse explains, "When a man and a woman in their differentiation and their complementarity see each other as truly other, yet the same as the self ('flesh of my flesh' [Genesis 2:20–23]), they are no longer bound only to previous kin relationships. They are invited to form new intimate bonds without guilt."[16] Gender differentiation and complementarity are essential to marriage, an institution he regards as based on the assumption that males and females are fundamentally different and yet attracted — by their gendered differences — to form complementary unions of two people who otherwise are incomplete. "The marriage bond," Stackhouse writes, "is a community of love between those who are 'other.' This means not simply 'an-other' person, but one who is truly 'other.'"[17] Two men or two women do not satisfy this essential requirement for gender difference and, therefore, complementarity.

Evangelical Christian ethicist Stanley J. Grenz argues similarly. To begin with, he notes that same-sex marriage is questionable definitionally. After all, in what proper sense of the word can it be said that a marriage of two men or of two women actually exists? "The obvious reason that such a relationship is not marriage," he writes, "arises from the fact that the partners are of the same sex. A homosexual union does not bring male and female together in an exclusive sexual bond." Because marriage by definition "involves the coming together of two people as sexual 'others' to form a new unity," it might appear as if two persons of the same sex could also unite. However, the uniting of two men or two women, Grenz asserts, is based on sexual sameness, not sexual differentiation or sexual otherness. Same-sex friendships are possible and desirable, but friendships are not sexual unions. In fact, sex between friends should never be encouraged because friendships are "generally neither an exclusive nor a formalized bond." Friendships symbolize "the inclusive, rather than the exclusive, love of God." This contrasts sharply with the sexualized union of two married partners. In marriage, Grenz argues, "the intent of the sex act . . . is to celebrate exclusivity, not inclusivity."[18]

Because gay people do not bring sexual *otherness* to their relationships, "a homosexual union can never fully be a uniting of the persons as two who are 'other' " in their sexuality. This lack of true otherness has theological significance. Same-sex unions by their nature cannot symbolize "what marriage is intended to convey: the reconciliation of otherness on the deepest level. Hence, because a homosexual relationship does not entail the uniting of the two foundational ways of being human, that is, as male and female, it does not appropriately symbolize human reconciliation. Nor can it connote the reconciliation of God and creation, who likewise are profoundly 'other' to each other."[19] Gay coupling can never be other than theologically inadequate.

Gayness as deficient

In addition to things *about marriage* that they believe bar same-sex couples from marrying, traditionalists identify things *about gay men and lesbians*, especially about their sexuality, that they insist further disqualify them as suitable "marriage material." Grenz argues against same-sex marriage by emphasizing the deficiency of gay sexuality. He allows how gay sex represents genital sexual expression that may approximate intimacy. However, gay sex is "not a complete expression of the sex act."[20] Gay marriage is, therefore, unethical because only (heterosexually) married people can engage in complete and, therefore, authentic sexual intercourse.

Gay sex will be forever deficient on at least two scores. First, sex between two men or two women lacks gender complementarity and cannot embody the one-flesh union that authentic marriage unions require. "At best," Grenz concludes, gay sex is "only a simulation of the two-becoming-one ritual that the act of sexual intercourse is designed to be." He quotes with approval James Hanigan's observation that "homosexual acts are ultimately 'only pretense or imaginary simulations of the real thing.' "[21] Second, gay sex is deficient because even if sex occurs within stable gay or lesbian relationships, it occurs within an improper context. The only proper context for sex is marriage, and marriage by definition is exclusively heterosexual. For a marriage to be authentic, it must bring together three essential meanings of human sexual intimacy: celebration of a lifelong commitment, mutuality of the partners, and procreative possibility. While same-sex relationships can meet the requirements of commitment and mutuality, they lack the procreative meaning. "At best," Grenz reiterates, "the act serves as an imitation of male-female procreative intercourse."[22]

The lack of procreative potential is not, finally, the ultimate reason for discounting same-sex unions as normative love relations. More troubling, Grenz argues, is that same-sex couples cannot express a full and exclusive sexual bonding, which he insists is the essence of the sex act's spiritual meaning. Heterosexual intercourse, characterized by the potential for or actual openness to procreation, "involves — and can only involve — two persons," he writes, a male and a female as potential biological parents. Because of this unique, biologically mandated bonding, male-female sex "provides a vivid symbolic declaration of the monogamous nature of the biblical ideal for marriage." In contrast, gay sex differs fundamentally because "there is nothing inherent in this physical act that would limit involvement to two persons." Grenz concludes: "In contrast to heterosexual intercourse, [gay sex] cannot function as the celebration of an exclusive bond and therefore cannot point to the exclusivity of the relationship God desires to have with us. In this way, same-sex intercourse loses the spiritual meaning of the sex act."[23] By its very nature, gay sex cannot embody or ritualize exclusivity, either human-human or human-divine.

Marriage traditionalists argue that even if lesbians and gay men form loving relationships, and even if the day comes when they will be allowed to marry legally, they will never truly "act married" because their coupling has no biologically based imperative for procreation and, therefore, no natural basis for monogamy and fidelity. Gay men, in particular, are judged incapable of monogamous relationships because they are, by their own choice, unmarried. Lacking wives, gay men have no reason, purportedly, not to enter into limitless sexual liaisons. Being unmarried and male means they are disconnected from any civilizing marriage context that could effectively manage to socialize them *as men*, requiring them to grow up, leave adolescence behind, and become responsible adults, sexually and socially.

According to this logic, the stabilizing function of marriage that restrains male sexual activity and channels it toward procreative ends eludes gay men entirely. The result is that because gay men are free of marital obligations (and also, presumably, of parenting responsibilities), they are free to be sexually uninhibited and irresponsible in terms of the number of partners. Their public "flaunting" of freedom from marriage, the major social control placed on sexuality in this culture, makes gay men the most visible nonconformists to the prevailing sex/gender regime.[24]

Fearful social consequences

Conservative commentator Stanley Kurtz explains the consequences for a society that allows "unbridled" (gay male) sexuality to go unchecked. Sexually transmitted diseases, including HIV/AIDS, become commonplace, but the worst consequence is the corruption of public morality. Once love and mutual pleasure become the sole criteria for sexual activity, no limits will be set, he fears. Marriage itself, the bedrock of civilization, will be replaced "by an infinitely flexible series of relationship contracts between persons of any number or gender." Where then will society be headed? Kurtz warns that "groups of three, four, and more will come before the public and the courts [in order to] demand recognition of their 'equal right' to a loving collective marriage." The push toward same-sex marriage will mean the actual dissolution of the institution of marriage. In its place, "we face legalized polygamy, group marriage, and the eventual legal abolition of marriage itself and its replacement by an infinitely flexible contract system."[25]

Marriage traditionalists foresee danger insofar as society is no longer willing to privilege "one man, one woman" marriage or restrict sexual activity to procreative heterosexual monogamy. The risk for changing the fundamental rules about marriage and sexuality, they warn, is sexual anarchy and social chaos. Critics of same-sex marriage link gay sexuality to the spread of disease, especially HIV/AIDS, and they speak of the health risks to both individuals and society.[26] They also emphasize that gayness places children in danger. At this point, conservatives run into trouble, precisely because a better-informed public no longer automatically equates gay men with pedophiles and the sexual abuse of children. In addition, because so many same-sex couples are raising children acquired either through adoption, alternative reproductive technologies, or previous heterosexual marriages, the conservative strategy has had to shift. Conservatives no longer get away with portraying gay men exclusively as sexual predators and pedophiles. Rather, they now insist that gay men and lesbians are deficient parents.[27]

Children are supposedly harmed by reason of living in households headed by adults of the same sex or by single parents. Alternative families are poor imitations of the (heterosexual) marital family because, among other things, they fail to socialize male and female children into their proper social and family roles as "normally" gendered males and females. Gay parents expose children to faulty gender and sexual modeling. Allowing gay men and lesbians to marry will only cause more suffering to untold numbers of "innocent victims," that is, to the children whose own sexual identity development will be impaired and whose lives will be disrupted because their families are different. Because of this difference, they are likely to be subjected to stigma and social ostracism.

Tradition gives no warrants for same-sex marriage

Normalization is a scare word for marriage traditionalists, opposed as they are to any effort to legitimate gay/lesbian sexuality, gay/lesbian

partnerships, and gay/lesbian families. Their final strategy against recognizing civil or religious marriage for same-sex couples is to argue
that tradition gives no warrant for such unions and validates heterosexual coupling alone. Max Stackhouse contends that extending the
right to marry to same-sex couples would be a radical, theologically
unwarranted departure from what he calls "the classical Christian
understanding" of "how God wants us to live."[28] Although Stackhouse
acknowledges both the intensity of the debates about sexuality within
Protestant churches and the changes that have taken place regarding
gender and family, he insists that a broad ecumenical consensus has
been sustained with respect to the exclusive normativity of heterosexuality and heterosexual marriage. As a marriage traditionalist,
Stackhouse insists that Christian marriage is only for heterosexuals.

In building his case, Stackhouse points out that most churches have
not wavered in their commitment to four basic affirmations. First, genital sex should be confined to heterosexual marriage alone. Second,
while churches should support human and civil rights for gay people,
this should be done without giving approval to "homosexual behavior" or same-sex marriage.[29] Third, "pastoral care for adults who are
single, gay, unable to procreate, or divorced is seen as morally and
spiritually required, even if their situations are not approved." Fourth,
although feminism has led to some modification in traditional theological and liturgical symbols, Stackhouse contends that feminism,
despite its increasing influence, has not changed "the basic teachings
about the normative character of the heterosexual family."[30] Together
these four claims form the core of what he calls a "classic tradition."
Not wavering from this tradition, he argues, is a matter of maintaining the integrity of Christian faith, "much in the way the ancient
prophets recalled the ancient covenants of God and adapted them to
changing situations."[31] Even when the call for change has come from
within religious communities, "the overall results of a quarter-century
of debate reflect a rejection of a radical effort to overturn the classical
position."[32]

In his own survey of recent church debates about homosexuality,
Grenz agrees with Stackhouse and other traditionalists that "the

North American church has come to a fork in the road in its understanding of sexuality and of the sex ethic it proclaims."[33] While the church should welcome all persons, including lesbians and gay men, and not hesitate to include them as church members, he recognizes that there is a division in the house over the morality of same-sex unions and, more specifically, over the morality of gay sex. To the question, "Is it proper for Christians to respond to homosexual urges by forming same-sex unions?" Grenz's answer is a definite no. The church must not condone sexual immorality. The standard for faithful Christians must be an ethic that restricts sex to heterosexual marriage and calls all others to abstinence. Joining the discipleship community must be done "on God's terms, not [our] own," Grenz concludes. "This entails being willing to leave behind old sinful practices — including unchaste sexual behaviors — so that together we might become a holy people."[34] A holy people will welcome gay people, so marriage traditionalists contend, but they will not affirm gay sex or gay unions.

Assessing the arguments against

The very first objection that conservative opponents raise against lesbian and gay marriage is definitional, that the standard meaning of the term "marriage" rules out the possibility of two men or two women marrying. When asked to account for the restriction, many opponents seem dumbfounded that they are being asked to defend, much less make a case for, something so obvious. Shouldn't it simply be taken for granted as the way things are, with no further explanation necessary? Furthermore, because common definitions are often circular and define marriage in terms of spouses, spouses in terms of husband and wife, and husband and wife in terms of marriage, they end up merely assuming what they promised at the outset to explain and, therefore, are seldom illuminating.

What is telling about the standard definitions of marriage is that they posit gender difference as the core structure of marriage. In popular culture, this bipolar gender pattern is expressed in terms of seeing men and women as "opposites," more dissimilar than similar to one another. Sexual interest and erotic desire are presumably sparked insofar as "opposites attract." This dualistic sex/gender framework serves as the underpinning for the binary character of Western thought and reflects how compulsory heterosexuality has become naturalized. However, despite claims that marriage is a natural or prepolitical institution, marriage has always been a socially constructed arrangement and subject to change.

Even with respect to gender, marriage has not been unalterable. Elements of marriage once considered essential have been questioned and judged unjust, such as a husband's ownership of his wife's property and the legal impossibility of a husband's raping his spouse. These notions are now widely discredited, largely because of the historic social justice movement for equality between men and women. Increased respect for women's equality and full moral personhood has also inspired a push to dismantle sexist patterns of male authority in family, church, and society. From a feminist perspective, marriage is ethically sound only when structured as a mutual partnership between two adults of equal legal and moral standing. In light of this, as Richard Mohr argues, "Now that gender distinctions have all but vanished from the legal *content* of marriage, there is no basis for the requirement that the legal *form* of marriage unite members of different sexes." The conventional one-man, one-woman definition of marriage has become "a dead husk that has been cast off by marriage as a living institution."[35]

The implications of this cultural shift toward gender equality and a degendered understanding of marriage are deeply troubling to marriage traditionalists. They fear that church and society may be moving in the direction of rejecting gender difference as the basic organizing principle for marriage and, by extension, all other social institutions. If good order requires not only gender difference, but also gender hierarchy, then men must be placed in charge and women be subordinate to male authority in the bedroom, the workplace, and throughout the public order. This male supremacist cultural paradigm perpetuates power differentials and maintains "man's world, woman's place,"[36] that is, a social order in which women's lives are secondary and derivative in relation to men's.

Traditionalists' claims about gender complementarity

Because it is no longer acceptable to speak, publicly at least, of women's inferiority, marriage traditionalists speak instead of gender complementarity as the necessary pattern for intimate and other social relations. Invoking this "complementarity" between men and women is code language for male power and female subordination socially, politically, economically, and sexually. Many such conventional theological claims about marriage mask gender injustice and do nothing to root out oppression. Given the strong leadership of women in the religious Right, language that connotes their inferiority must be suppressed in favor of "softer" language that merely suggests that men and women have significant role differences, a variation on the separate-but-equal theme. However, as religious feminists point out, there is little doubt that the "overarching issue is the defense of traditional gender hierarchy in patriarchal marriage."[37]

Even though men and women are equal spiritually, "in the flesh" a good woman keeps her place and remains compliant (or at least not openly rebellious) toward male authority. Her goodness depends upon her being feminine, that is, socially dependent and sexually available to her husband. Similarly, a good man, defined as overtly heterosexual and masculine, is a good worker and husband. He fulfills his duty by working hard, even at jobs that are low paying, demeaning, and dangerous, and by claiming his rightful position at home over "his" woman and "his" children. Even when that control is presented as benign protection and care of his dependents, the underlying structure is one of male power over others, the perfect setup for domestic violence, as the feminist movement has analyzed for more than three decades.[38]

In a globalizing economy with its ever widening inequalities and major restructuring of work and family life, increasing numbers of men are struggling with a crisis in masculinity as they confront unemployment, underemployment, and the necessity of having a wage-earning wife to subsidize the family's economy. One of the ways a man may compensate for his increased economic and social dependency is by asserting his "God-given" sexist and heterosexist privilege, a strategy that the Christian Right reinforces in its "traditional family values" campaign and anti-gay rhetoric. Although a man may not be the successful economic provider he wishes for his family, at least he does not shirk his patriarchal responsibilities by "turning queer" or exploiting public assistance through the welfare system. In this paradigm, heterosexuality represents compliance not only to conventional patterns of male-female exchange, but to an entire cultural paradigm of family, work, and community life. The Christian Right reinforces the notion of heterosexual marriage as what "normality" means for men and women, as well as good citizenship. Repudiating gayness and asserting male authority in the family are twin components of a cultural configuration that is then securely fastened by eroticizing male control of women as sexy and titillating.[39] "Real" men desire dominance, both over women and socially subordinate men, and "real" women desire to be dominated.

For these reasons, traditionalists regard extending legal recognition and religious affirmation to same-sex relationships as ominous steps. They fear that degendering marriage will make the entire social order gender neutral. They see other negative developments contributing to this fearful outcome, including no-fault divorce, single parenting, and the expansion within the last three decades of women's public and economic roles. At the same time, conservative appeals to holding fast to a conventional definition (and practice) of marriage have not stopped the cultural momentum. Positing marriage as a natural, nonpolitical institution has not blocked further change of the (heterosexual) marital family paradigm. Paradoxically, conservatives undermine their own case for marriage as a fixed, unalterable institution insofar as they insist, on the one hand, that the patriarchal family is natural and, on the other hand, that it requires special privileging in order to survive.[40]

The disparagement of same-sex love and eroticism

To stem the tide against further gender changes in marriage, traditionalists insist on drawing a line to prevent those they regard as the quintessential gender nonconformists from gaining state recognition or religious blessing of their unions. Gay sexuality is caricatured not so much by inferiorizing stereotypes as immoralizing ones.[41] First, same-sex sexual desire is described as perverse and likened to bestiality. Second, gay people are defined exclusively by their (unnatural) sexuality, as if gayness is a master trait that overrides all other human characteristics and, therefore, distorts their very humanity, turning it into something deviant and terribly wrong.

This sexualizing of gay men and lesbians is reductionistic, misguided, and demeaning. "Our partners are not walking dildos and vibrators," Jonathan Rauch bluntly states. "Our partners are our companions, our soulmates, *our loves.*"[42] Moreover, a homophobic, repressively violent society has never encouraged lesbians and gay men to form committed relationships, nor has it recognized the validity of same-sex love by granting the right to marry. Stigmatized as emotionally immature, gay people are viewed as incapable of love. Their humanness has been reduced to sex alone. The message far and wide has been that homoerotically attracted persons are capable of nothing better than furtive, fleeting sexual encounters with anonymous partners.

Given the cultural disparagement and violent persecution of same-sex love, what is remarkable is that gay men and lesbians have managed, against these odds, to form significant intimate relationships. Many have developed long-lasting networks of friends and lovers. Although LBGT people have not had the option to marry, they have successfully created alternative, nonmarital families and other networks of affection, support, and care.[43]

In responding to the allegation that gay people are relational failures and notoriously promiscuous, Rauch inquires, "Exactly how monogamous do homosexuals have to be in order to earn the right to marry?" If two men or two women are refused the right to marry "because we're not as sexually well behaved as married heterosexuals," why is it, he continues, that "no matter how badly heterosexuals behave, their right to marry will go unquestioned? Really, the gall!"[44]

Conservative arguments that gay people are not only outsiders, but also threats to family, may carry weight in this culture, given the strong presumption that family means a heterosexual unit with two parents, one male and the other female. However, current social scientific research does not support their claims that children lose if raised by a gay parent or in a same-sex household. In a 1995 comprehensive review of the research literature for the American Psychological Association, researcher Charlotte J. Patterson acknowledges that beliefs about lesbians and gay men as unfit parents are commonplace, but they "have no empirical foundation."[45] She debunks the notion that children's best interests are served by keeping a parent's sexual identity as lesbian or gay secret. She also challenges the "wisdom" that a lesbian or gay parent should raise children in a separate household and not be seen "fraternizing" with a same-sex partner.[46] In her summary Patterson notes, "Not a single study has found children of gay or lesbian parents to be disadvantaged in any significant respect relative to children of heterosexual parents. Indeed, the evidence to date suggests that home environments provided by gay and lesbian parents are as likely as those provided by heterosexual parents to support and enable children's psychosocial growth."[47] The difficulties that these children may encounter have as their source not their family structure, but rather the cultural homophobia which views anything gay in a negative light.

In truth, there is something different about lesbian and gay families. LBGT-headed families are different from the cultural norm, especially insofar as same-sex partners typically share parental responsibilities more equally and trade family roles more fluidly than their heterosexual counterparts. The research data indicate that the equal sharing of childcare duties is something positive, associated "with more advantageous outcomes for both parents and for children."[48] Building on these research findings, legal scholars argue that legalizing marriage for same-sex couples with children would have an overall positive effect on other families, as well as their own. Having access to marital status would allow a nonbiological gay or lesbian parent to adopt his or her partner's offspring. Gaining marriage benefits under the law would strengthen and further stabilize same-sex relationships for the long term. In case of a breakup, divorce laws would provide safeguards for the care of dependent children and protect their economic interests. Finally, children of gay parents who could marry "would see their family as 'more normal.'"[49]

An oppositional difference paradigm

Throughout their negative discourse about same-sex marriage, marriage traditionalists construct their arguments on the basis of an oppositional difference paradigm that presumes heterosexual unions are different from and superior to same-sex unions, just as heterosexuality is different from and superior to homosexuality. In an exercise of stunted epistemology, the experiences and witness of gay people are never taken into account. Rather, gay people are objectified as the Other, whose lives and love threaten the stability and status of the cultural majority. The abstraction "homosexuality" lies at the center of their discourse. Gay people — or rather "homosexuals" — are talked about and spoken to, but they are not listened to or learned from, nor is their moral authority taken into account as co-shapers of religious and moral tradition.

Marriage traditionalists make essentialist claims about sexuality, marriage, and same-sex relations without appreciation for the diversity and complexity of gay lives, including the diversity and complexity of gay sexuality. Equally problematic is making moral judgments on the basis of an entire category of persons. Finally, marriage traditionalists miss entirely a salient characteristic of the social and sexual pluralism within U.S. culture. As Frank Kameny notes, "In point of fact, homosexuality is far more a matter of love and affection than it is commonly considered to be; and heterosexuality is far more a matter of physical lust than our culture, with its over-romanticized approach, admits it to be. Actually, homosexuality and heterosexuality differ but little, if at all, in this respect."[50]

Viewing heterosexuality and homosexuality as binary opposites reinforces heterosexual supremacy, the conviction that heterosexuality alone is normative for organizing intimate relations and family life. A moral divide is posited between heterosexuality (good sex) and homosexuality (bad or deficient sex). The circularity of the argument that marriage by definition excludes same-sex couples and that marriage is necessarily a heterosexual institution begs the question at debate, namely, whether same-sex love is morally comparable to heterosexual love and, therefore, deserving of the same support, benefits, and protections that male-female couples receive.

Appeals to a static, unalterable Christian marriage tradition fail to take into account the pluralistic and conflicted character of Christianity itself. As Rosemary Ruether points out, Christianity has had a "volatile relationship" throughout its history to the family. "Modern Christians think Christianity has always championed 'the family,' but this belief ignores three-fourths of actual Christian history."[51] For many centuries, the church had a negative or at least ambivalent attitude about marriage, to be discussed further in chapter 6. Historically speaking, Christianity has been anti-family for much of the time. The fixation with so-called family values and with the preservation of the marital family is a recent development, not at all reflective of much previous Christian sentiment.

The Protestant Reformation in the sixteenth century precipitated a reevaluation of marriage. In the modern period, marriage has been viewed largely as a "creational ordinance demanded of all" and as a "necessary means to control the lustful urges of fallen 'man.' "[52] When the Christian Right speaks of "upholding tradition," the tradition they seek to defend is short-lived. Moreover, like all tradition, it is constructed and, therefore, subject to debate and revision. What they lift up as normative is a nineteenth-century Victorian model of white, middle-class marriage in which the husband works outside the home and the wife is a full-time homemaker. Thus, the marriage tradition they endorse is not only historically bounded; it is also a radical departure from the church's message for more than fifteen hundred years, namely, that "marriage is a second-class choice for Christians."[53]

Contrary to essentialist claims about marriage or a heterosexual definition of marriage as nondebatable, marriage is an evolving institution whose meanings have been long contested, as they are being contested once again. As E. J. Graff acknowledges, cultural conservatives complain that "changing a given rule changes the very *definition* of marriage. And of course, they're right."[54] Once a patriarchal theory of male supremacy and female inferiority is discredited, and once marriage is valued primarily as a protective, stabilizing context for intimacy and ongoing care between partners, then justifications for excluding same-sex partners melt away. In light of these transformations, new definitions and institutional forms inevitably emerge.

Revising the definition of marriage

Roman Catholic moral theologian Daniel Maguire offers this revised definition of marriage: "Marriage is the highest form of interpersonal commitment and friendship achievable between sexually attracted persons."[55] This definition requires neither heterosexual coupling nor procreative possibility. Furthermore, a distinction is drawn between the goods of marriage that are indispensable and must be evident for a marriage to be recognizable as a marriage, and those goods of marriage that are dispensable. Offspring may and often do enhance marital life, but children are not essential for fulfilling the marriage covenant. Furthermore, children are the only good related specifically to heterosexuality, but that claim should be further qualified, given the availability of adoption and assisted reproductive technologies to single women, infertile heterosexual couples, and same-sex couples. Many same-sex couples are also parenting.

The indispensable moral goods of marriage are companionship, mutual trust, and care. None is a function of gender or sexual orientation. These goods of marriage include the "total acceptance of all aspects of the self," the experience of creative loving, and the opportunity to be nurtured in a "school of holiness where persons may grow closer to God as they grow closer to one another and where their conjugal love may fuel their passion for justice and love for all people."[56]

Traditionalists' arguments against same-sex marriage pivot on their disapproval of gay sex and their denial that same-sex love is morally comparable to heterosexual love. A progressive Christian ethic, in contrast, honors eroticism, both gay and non-gay, as a source of power and energy that suffuses not only sexual activity, but also life pursuits more broadly. We humans, in our sexual and social diversity, share a remarkably similar desire for connection, communication, and communion with other persons, with the earth, and with God. Although the erotic is a dimension of human existence, this does not mean that marriage or sex is necessary for human fulfillment. However, it does mean that it is wrong to exclude an entire class of persons from these routes to intimacy and shared pleasure. "The desire for a significant other with whom we are uniquely conjoined," Maguire concludes, "is not a heterosexual but a basic human desire. The programmatic exclusion of gay persons from the multiple benefits of erotic attraction, which often opens the way to such a union, is arbitrary, harmful, cruel, and therefore sinful."[57]

To claim, as marriage traditionalists do, that, on the one hand, homosexual sex is incomplete and deficient and, on the other hand, that only heterosexual persons can experience the fullness of love, reinforces compulsory heterosexuality. In contrast, an egalitarian framework, informed by feminist and LBGT liberation perspectives, questions the basic categories of gender and sexual differentiation that devalue sexual diversity and support heterosexual supremacy. All persons, male and female, share the capacity for psychological wholeness and moral self-direction. Once the assumptions of gender complementarity and of "oppositions attracting" no longer hold, then it is possible to affirm the goodness of all sexual and social relations based on respect and mutual care.

That the underlying purpose of marriage is "to protect and encourage the union of committed couples," and that the law should recognize the validity of unions between two men or two women is the conclusion reached in 1999 by the Vermont Supreme Court. The Vermont justices situated their legal decision in continuity with the long-term historical movement toward equalizing the status of marriage partners.[58] In ruling in favor of the lesbian and gay plaintiffs seeking marriage licenses, the justices noted that "their [the plaintiffs'] claim is simply and fundamentally for inclusion in the family of state-sanctioned human relations."[59] To grant equal legal access to marriage benefits and protections, the Court concluded, is "simply, when all is said and done, a recognition of our common humanity."[60]

Lessons for the justice struggle

This inquiry into the opposition among marriage traditionalists, including the Christian Right, to same-sex marriage has yielded at least three key insights. First, justice requires affirming a common humanity that is shared by all persons, male and female, heterosexual and nonheterosexual alike. Denial of that oneness is wrong. Differential treatment of persons merely on the basis of gender or sexuality is wrong, especially unequal treatment that perpetuates a fundamental dividing line between "us" and "them" and strengthens the position of the privileged group.[61]

Second, the politics of cultural change are complicated and may result in unintended consequences. Although those engaged in an aggressive politics of preservation have, to date, successfully prevented the extension of civil marriage rights to lesbians and gay men, they have failed to meet their primary objective, namely, to keep marriage central to the culture and in a uniquely privileged place. Because of their determination not to recognize the validity of same-sex relationships or include them within the marriage circle, they have inadvertently helped to multiply the number of institutionalized alternatives outside of marriage that are now available to same-sex couples, including reciprocal beneficiaries (Hawaii), civil unions (Vermont), and domestic partnerships, recognized in numerous state and local municipalities and by hundreds of corporations. These alternatives give significant legal standing to same-sex couples even though they continue to lack the full standing that marriage provides. Moreover, because these alternatives to marriage are available (in most jurisdictions) to heterosexual couples as well, marriage traditionalists may have "saved" marriage for heterosexuals only, but they have also "succeeded" in further decentering marriage for everyone in light of the proliferation of these other options.

A third lesson is about the power of language and, in this instance, of the word "marriage." Marriage seems an almost enchanted term that has been reserved for the most highly prized sexual and intimate affiliations. While the Vermont civil union legislation grants lesbian and gay couples the same legal rights and benefits of marriage that heterosexual couples enjoy, it does not grant the use of the name. For marriage advocates, gaining all the perks but not the status is, as David Chambers laments, "in honesty, a fairly pallid package. What counts most is the name."[62]

Over twenty-five years ago, a progressive Christian ethicist suggested that the most difficult question of all for the churches to resolve would be the notion of same-sex marriage because of the negativity about homosexuality and because of the power of symbols. In the dominant religious (and cultural) imagination, marriage has been consistently associated with heterosexuality and, as noted, with male-dominant/female-subordinate bonds. Acceptance of marriage for same-sex couples would be, this ethicist predicted, "a long time off." In the meantime, churches should press for liturgical support of gay unions and civil recognition as a matter of fundamental justice.[63]

Chapter 4 examines the arguments put forward by advocates of same-sex marriage who believe strongly that the time is no longer "far off," but rather has now come to extend the freedom to marry to same-sex couples.

CHAPTER FOUR

Marriage Advocates

Same-sex commitments are nothing new;
only the demand for equity and recognition
have changed the landscape.[1]

— ELLEN LEWIN

A vehicle for normalization?

Advocates of extending marriage eligibility to same-sex couples have no bone to pick with marriage traditionalists when it comes to marriage. They, too, are enthusiastic about marriage and acknowledge its key role as a stabilizing social institution. They, too, privilege marriage as the favored site for sustaining committed intimate relationships and fostering vibrant families. They, too, call on church and state to bolster the status of marriage as the primary building block of a strong society.

Where same-sex marriage advocates and marriage traditionalists part company is not over marriage, but over homosexuality. Those in favor of same-sex marriage regard gayness as a morally good, perfectly valid way of being human. They seek public recognition of and support for lesbian and gay marriages as a way to validate and gain protection for LBGT partnerships and families. They also insist that there is nothing radical in allowing gays to marry. As theologian Jack Rogers, a former moderator of the Presbyterian Church (U.S.A.), puts the matter, "I don't care what you call it — marriage, domestic partnership, holy union. It is not the form I am interested in but the function. It seems to me that it is in the best interest of the state, and of the church, to recognize and encourage persons who are willing to make life-long commitments to each other and to children they raise." At the same time, he notes, "In a culture of non-marriage it is very ironic that we are spending great amounts of money and energy in trying to prevent people from marrying who want to do so in a way that would contribute to the stability of society."[2]

Contrary to the sentiments expressed by the religious Right and other anti-gay conservatives, the British journal *The Economist* has editorialized that gayness is nothing dangerous, that same-sex marriage does not threaten the centrality of that institution, and that the vast majority of gay people are both in the mainstream and committed to mainstream values, including the marital family. Moreover, cultural change with respect to human sexuality and sexual difference is well underway, such that heterosexuals are becoming more aware of their homosexual counterparts whose chant might be, "We're here, we're queer, we're boring." "Across the world," *The Economist* contends, "a radical idea about homosexuals is gaining ground: they are like, say, left-handers, a very ordinary minority." The journal promotes this theme in an editorial entitled "Let Them Wed" and also through visual art. The journal's front cover depicts a tiered wedding cake topped with figurines of a happy wedding couple: two men (white and apparently middle-class professionals, no doubt similar to the readership of the journal) dressed in tuxedos and holding hands. In case readers miss the point, an inside story announces, "Moreover, it's normal to be queer."[3]

If marriage traditionalists fear nothing more than the normalization of gayness and the public validation of same-sex families, advocates of same-sex marriage want nothing more than to mainstream lesbians and gay men as everyday people who deserve the same respect and rights as other citizens. This chapter examines their case for same-sex marriage and begins by considering how the marriage paradigm itself is changing. Many have come to view marriage as a partnership between equals in which commitment, not gender and not predetermined gender roles, is central. Moral discourse about marriage is being further recast because LBGT people are entering the conversation, claiming their authority as reformers in behalf of "intimate democracy," and bringing their outsiders' wisdom to bear on family life. After detailing the advocates' arguments in support of same-sex marriage and their counter-arguments to the objections of marriage traditionalists, this chapter assesses the case for same-sex marriage in light of a progressive Christian ethical commitment to promote sexual and gender justice.

Intimate democracy

Advocates of same-sex marriage insist that marriage traditionalists are misguided not only about homosexuality, but also about marriage insofar as they assume that marriage requires two "complementary" genders within an authority structure that places the husband in charge. In an essay entitled "Are Family Values Enduring Values?" Patricia Smith contends that while the conventional patriarchal construction of the marital family is now widely critiqued, certain values remain highly prized with respect to family and other intimate relations. These include responsibility, cooperation, care, loyalty, love, support, and "identification with the interests of certain special others as equal to your own." Such values "apparently endure," Smith notes, but the social structures within which they are lived out are constantly changing and evolving.[4]

In this regard, the global feminist movement is of particular significance. It aims to improve the status of women everywhere and press for recognition of women's moral autonomy. Because of women's rising expectations for enhanced economic and cultural power, increasing numbers of women (and men) are no longer content with traditional patriarchal patterns. At the same time, Smith underscores, "The commitment to family living or at least to long-term committed relationships is still predominant as an ideal."[5] What the feminist revolution calls for is not the demise of the family, but rather its reorganization based on respect for women's humanity and their human rights.

In a recent study of lesbian and gay families, sociologist Jeffrey Weeks and two colleagues observe that a new relational norm is emerging in relation to intimate life. Many gay (and non-gay) adults are seeking personal fulfillment within a context of egalitarian re-lationships that are freely chosen, what they describe as emotional or intimate democracy.[6] Their in-depth interviews with nearly one hundred LBGT people, half men and half women, identify three core values of same-sex relationships: personal choice, sexual compatibility, and mutual trust. This egalitarian model suggests that a transforma-tion of intimate life is underway from the cultural underside. However, because of differentials of power even between same-sex partners, this ideal is difficult to attain. "The reality is often complex," Weeks writes, and yet "the egalitarian relationship *has* become a measure by which people seek to judge their individual lives."[7]

In this culture, as noted in chapter 1, consent is regarded as cru-cial for marriage. Although marriage is about many things, including economics, raising children, and mutual aid in times of trouble, it is fundamentally also about mutual affection, respect, and the desire of the two people to marry for love. Because of this strong cultural asso-ciation of marriage with love and personal choice, marriage advocates argue that the denial of marriage to lesbians and gay men is unjust because the prohibition is inconsistent with this widely shared commit-ment to choice in intimate life. Given the centrality of consent, doesn't it make sense to prioritize choice even over gender in defining the es-sentials of marriage? The delinking of marriage from gender and of sex from procreation marks a larger, quite profound cultural transforma-tion toward gender equality and women's (and men's) emancipation from fixed social and familial roles. If heterosexual people can freely marry the person they love, why shouldn't gay people also be free to marry whom they love?

Given the centrality of marriage to this culture, many LBGT people regard their exclusion from marriage as offensive, regardless of whether they themselves would ever choose to marry. Jonathan Rauch writes, "To be prohibited from taking a spouse is not a minor inconvenience. It is a lacerating deprivation."[8] Andrew Sullivan argues similarly: "De-nial of marriage to gay people is . . . the most profound statement our society can make that homosexual love is simply not as good as hetero-sexual love; that gay lives and commitments and hopes are simply worth less." This marriage exclusion "erases them not merely as citizens, but as human beings."[9] Correcting this public affront, he insists, is "ultimately the only reform that truly matters."[10]

From a liberal human rights perspective, the freedom to choose a marital (or nonmarital) partner is a person-defining choice with which the state should not interfere.[11] Denying marriage rights to an entire class of persons is morally suspect, especially because the primary obstacles to extending marriage rights to same-sex couples are social discrimination and negative stereotyping. Granting gays the right to marry would offer LBGT people relief from an injustice, but it would have additional social benefits, as well. Marriage would normalize or "mainstream" participating LBGT couples. Along these lines, Martha Nussbaum writes, "Encouraging gay marriages will help to remove stereotypes of gays as promiscuous and culturally subversive." Furthermore, marriage will help promote family and social stability, another strong reason to proceed in this direction.[12]

A *human rights struggle*

Rethinking marriage and sexuality requires openness to new perspectives and alternative knowledge within the context of struggles for gender and sexual justice. An epistemological shift is called for that involves listening deeply and respectfully to LBGT people and learning how they manage to sustain intimate partnerships within a hostile culture. If the traditional marital family is in crisis, then those forced to live outside its protective confines can speak knowledgeably about new challenges and new possibilities. This insight accords with an insight central to progressive, justice-centered theologies discussed in chapter 2, that taking the "view from below" — the perspective of the marginalized and oppressed — offers a corrective lens for viewing socially constructed reality in contrast to the "official truths" presented by the beneficiaries of the status quo.

The attentiveness within the LBGT community to intimate relationships and families has come about, in part, as a response to the HIV/AIDS pandemic. This politically charged health crisis has vividly demonstrated how the lack of full citizenship rights and legal protections for primary partnerships only makes vulnerable people's lives more difficult, from securing hospital visitation rights to gaining health insurance coverage for a life partner. Lesbian and gay parents have also had to struggle, often in courts of law, to defend their active involvement with their children, as well as their eligibility for foster parenting and adoption. A lesbian and gay "baby boom" of sorts seems to be occurring in the LBGT community, as increasing numbers of couples are raising children from previous (heterosexual) marriages, because of adoption, or by means of assisted reproductive technologies. For this reason, more LBGT people have become concerned about securing the political, economic, and legal conditions to safeguard their families.

In the midst of their efforts to sustain families despite oppression, LBGT people have had to become inventors of alternative models. No maps are available to provide directions about how to live outside the heterosexual paradigm. With creativity the LBGT community has developed extended "tribes" of friends and loved ones who provide support, assistance, and stability to one another, especially when their biological families reject them or fail to respond to their needs. Because these networks are not automatically available but must be constantly reinvented, they require a reflective self-awareness and intentionality beyond what is required of most heterosexual couples. In *Our Families, Our Values: Snapshots of Queer Kinship*, Robert Goss and Amy Strongheart describe these alternative networks as "the relationships we hold dear and that we recognize as sacred and familial."[13]

To be sure, the quest for intimate democracy is an unfinished revolution, and yet over the course of a single generation, a gay rights/liberation movement has made it possible for LBGT people to live openly and organize to pursue legal rights. Increasing numbers of people are going public about their desire to partner with a person of the same-sex and marry "their own kind." All this indicates a strong self-confidence and creative energy within the LBGT community.

The conventional wisdom has been that "kinship and all that it is thought to entail — intense, unconditional bonds of love and lifelong commitment as well as the mundane details of domesticity — cannot be a part of gay life."[14] The alternative wisdom "from the underside" is that LBGT persons are adept at forming and sustaining families and intimate partnerships. For this reason, marriage advocates, in noting the vibrancy of same-sex relationships in their racial, economic, and cultural diversity, contend that LBGT people have every right to use the same vocabulary that non-gays use to speak of love, family, and commitment. Legal activist Evan Wolfson writes, "It is the vocabulary of love, equality, and inclusion."[15] This vocabulary is the language LBGT people use to describe their lives, and it should be the vocabulary that non-gays employ when speaking about LBGT lives. Anglican theologian Robert Williams has argued similarly that marriage between two men or two women should be called marriage, not holy unions or some other term. "A covenanted relationship between two women or two men is just as much a Christian *marriage* as that between a man and a woman," he writes, "and the only way to overcome this visceral reaction to the term 'gay marriage' is to make a point of using it frequently."[16]

When LBGT persons are listened to with respect as subjects, what may be learned about love and intimacy? At least three insights are worth mentioning.

First, LBGT people exist. They are fully human. They love. They create families and relationships of value.

Second, with respect to this capacity for human intimacy, gay and non-gay people are morally equivalent. In *The Morality of Gay Rights*, Carlos Ball emphasizes that sexuality is intrinsic to any person's humanity: "The morally relevant point is that lesbians and gay men have needs and capabilities for physical and emotional intimacy and that those needs and capabilities — as expressed through their sexuality and their love and care of others — help define them as human beings."[17] Because sexuality is a defining trait of a person's full humanity, it merits moral respect. What is morally irrelevant is the gender of the person one loves or with whom one partners.

Third, the marriage question should be reframed. The question is not whether lesbians and gay men are worthy of recognition or whether their intimate partnerships should be protected. Rather, it should be asked repeatedly how church and society can enhance social conditions so that same-sex relationships and families can thrive. Because a good society guarantees the conditions for its members to flourish, isn't there a social obligation to create the conditions that will allow LBGT people to flourish *as LBGT people?* On this score, more from the state is needed than merely protecting individuals from discrimination or desisting from state-authorized coercion. The conditions for LBGT flourishing must be promoted to enable flourishing according to *their* conceptions of the humanly good.[18] This shifts the focus away from a preoccupation with privacy rights (the freedom to be left alone) to a concern for promoting associational or relational rights. Insofar as the state is obligated to encourage only behaviors recognized as good, the question becomes, are same-sex relationships (recognized as) morally good and valuable?

Marriage advocates realize that the struggle for LBGT liberation is larger than ending discrimination in employment and housing, larger than stopping anti-gay violence, and larger even than securing certain rights, including the right to marry, important as these are. The bigger struggle is for social equality and the recognition of LBGT people as fully human subjects of their own lives, worthy of respect, care, and protection by the communities in which they live. Recognizing the humanity of LBGT people is the central message of the ruling by the Vermont State Supreme Court in its *Baker v. Vermont* decision granting the same rights and benefits to same-sex couples that currently belong to married heterosexual couples. "The past provides many instances where the law refused to see a human being when it should have," the justices write.[19] Recognizing the humanity of lesbians and gay men means, among other things, that lesbians and gay men should also be perceived as the marrying kind.

Framing the case in favor

A GLAD (Gay and Lesbian Advocates and Defenders) publication offers three reasons that marriage matters. First, marriage is "a major building block for strong families and communities." Second, marriage is the access point for hundreds of protections and benefits from state and federal government. Third, marriage is a basic right of citizenship, and to be denied the right to marry means that "gay men and lesbians will continue to fall short of the status of full citizenship, marking them and their children with a stamp of inferiority."[20]

About the state's interest in marriage, Michael Wald at Stanford Law School identifies four concerns. First, marriage law encourages people to enter into long-term, stable relationships, especially if there are children. (Divorce laws, on the other hand, have been designed to make termination of these relationships anything but quick and easy.) Second, the state promotes marriage as an economic sharing between two adults not only for their benefit, but also for the benefit of the state insofar as independent marital units have less need for direct economic subsidies. Third, many people find that their emotional well-being is enhanced through marriage. To have citizens nurtured and cared for in their daily lives is a desirable social outcome. Fourth, marriage plays a role in creating an open democratic society. "In marriage people learn to define themselves," Wald writes, "as caring rather than egoistic beings, as connected to, rather than alienated from, the concerns and well-being of others. As a result, they are more likely to give to society."[21]

Because these reasons also apply to same-sex couples, marriage advocates insist that marriage should apply to lesbian and gay partnerships, as well. The further presumption is that it is advantageous to make marriage available to as many people as possible. Society would be strengthened, not weakened, by making marriage more inclusive.

About the interest of religious traditions in same-sex marriage, theologian Rebecca Alpert, speaking from a Reconstructionist Jewish perspective, observes that many faith communities, including her own, support same-sex marriage. Religious leaders have performed union services, including those from the Universal Fellowship of Metropolitan Community Churches, the Society of Friends, the United Church of Christ, and the Unitarian Universalist Association, as well as Lutheran, Presbyterian, and United Methodist clergy, Episcopal and Roman Catholic priests, and Reform and Reconstructionist rabbis.

Not all performed these services with the approval of their denominations, but, nonetheless, they acted in their capacity as ordained leaders. Some have conducted very public ceremonies involving hundreds of couples at LBGT national marches on Washington in 1987 and 1992. Alpert argues that "if religious denominations are willing to perform same-sex marriages they ought to have the right to confer the same societal benefits for those marriages as for those of heterosexuals." However, religious ceremonies do not confer legal status, and clergy, even though designated agents of the state, are not the final arbiters of civil marriage laws.[22]

Religious traditions offer multiple grounds for supporting marriage for same-sex couples. The values of economic justice, committed partnership, and care of children apply to same-sex couples. Although marriage was historically viewed as an exchange of property in which the woman was passed from father to husband, the economics of marriage has changed with the political and economic emancipation of women. Marriage still retains economic significance, and for many same-sex couples, as for many heterosexual couples, a prime motivation to marry is economic.

Two other values give further reasons for supporting same-sex marriage rights. First, marriage is about the love, commitment, and faithful partnership of two persons whom the religious community blesses and supports in their union. Again, a contemporary revision of marriage sensibilities emphasizes that it is no longer the exclusive duty of the husband to earn the money or the wife's sole obligation to tend to the household. Rather, marriage is an equal partnership between interdependent parties. Second, religion values children, including children in lesbian and gay families who arrive through adoption, alternative reproductive techniques, and oftentimes through previous heterosexual unions.[23]

The religious values of economic justice, committed love, and procreation are as central for same-sex couples as they are for other-sex couples. What makes marriage meaningful is the centrality of these values, not a particular gender configuration. Other advocates make a similar case. The extending of marriage rights to same-sex couples is seen as a matter of basic fairness and treating similarly situated cases alike. Protestant theologian Karen Lebacqz writes, "Marriage ceremonies do not create marriages but bear witness to an already existing marriage. Hence, to allow ceremonies for heterosexual couples but prohibit them for gay and lesbian couples is unjust: it constitutes discrimination."[24] Treating two classes of persons differently is discriminatory, and such exclusionary laws "degrade the human person because they create, ipso facto, a 'second class' citizenship for gay and lesbian people in the church."[25]

Same-sex couples should also be afforded the same opportunity as heterosexual couples to succeed — or fail — at marriage. Since many heterosexuals do a less than sterling job of marriage, some advocates argue, tongue in cheek, that same-sex couples should have equal opportunity to do as poorly as their heterosexual counterparts. Others emphasize that lesbian and gay couples deserve an opportunity to be seen as "maritally competent." Everyone deserves the chance, Jonathan Rauch writes, "to participate in society's most important civic institution. At a bare minimum, if the [fear] is that homosexuals will wreck marriage, we should not be forever denied any hope of showing that we won't wreck marriage."[26]

In defining the issue as equal access, advocates seek to calm the fears of those who worry that allowing lesbians and gay men to marry will devalue marriage or cause further instability in family life. Michael Wald insists that authorizing marriage for same-sex couples will only bring more people into the institution but "not change its fundamental elements."[27] Marriage reform is, therefore, presented as an expansion of the pool of eligible persons, not as an altering of the institution itself. The goal is equal access, not the transformation of marriage into something different.

Answering the objections

Objections to same-sex marriage fall under four headings: definitional claims, moral objections, reasonable alternatives, and likely consequences. Advocates of same-sex marriage, in seeking to set these objections aside, make a counter-argument: because marriage is a basic human right, it should not be denied lesbians and gay men unless there is a compelling reason, which proponents are certain does not exist.

Definitional claims: Contrary to essentialist claims that marriage is a timeless institution unchanged over the course of thousands of years, marriage is a socially constructed and contested institution that has changed in the past and is subject now to further modification. The strength of this institution is its adaptability. This means, among other things, that there is no static universal definition of marriage. If marriage were still seen as a patriarchal property arrangement with specific social and family roles assigned by gender, then a same-sex union would not be conceivable as a marriage. However, according to contemporary definition, marriage is something quite different: a partnership of equals based on mutual love and caring. By this definition, same-sex couples qualify.

Other advocates challenge the definitional objections to same-sex marriage by claiming, as William Eskridge does in his monograph "The History of Same-Sex Marriage," that there is nothing novel or radical about committed lesbian and gay partnerships. In fact, such unions are traditional and ordinary. "Same-sex unions have been a valuable institution for most of human history and in most known cultures," Eskridge writes. Furthermore, "most societies we know anything about — including the West — have recognized same-sex unions, usually including same-sex marriages at various points in their history."[28] What has changed is not the fact of gay unions, but rather the (heterosexual majority) public's recognition of their existence and value.

Moral objections: If marriage traditionalists' concern is to preserve family values, advocates of same-sex marriage point out that some of these so-called traditional values have been oppressive toward women and LBGT people and should be critiqued, not perpetuated. Just as marriage is socially constructed, so, too, moral traditions are constructions that are historically situated and contestable. If settled conventions cause harm, they should be altered. (Chapter 6 addresses how religious traditions are being challenged by their own membership to reverse a troubling legacy of sexual oppression and discrimination.)

Although marriage traditionalists cite morality as their primary reason for refusing to legitimate same-sex relationships, marriage advocates argue that morality is on the side of doing justice and showing respect for LBGT partnerships. What is wrong morally is discrimination and barring an entire class of persons from exercising a fundamental human right without compelling reason. What journalist Anna Quindlen has written about sodomy laws and other punitive anti-gay restrictions applies, as well, to the legal proscriptions that deny marriage to same-sex couples: "The sodomy laws are part of a dark tradition in this nation; they do not exist, and have never existed, to serve the public weal. They are meant only to demonize and marginalize a class of human beings." No laws, including federal and state DOMAs (Defense of Marriage Act), are morally justified insofar as they "exist purely for the purpose of codifying and justifying bigotry."[29]

If exclusion is wrong, advocates are also certain that including same-sex couples within the institution of marriage is morally right. Carlos Ball makes an explicitly moral argument in favor of same-sex marriage in an essay entitled "That We Are Human, We Have Rights." "Most gay rights issues implicate, in one form or another, the human capacity to love others. Whether we like it or not," Ball writes, "we cannot avoid questions of [morality and] what it means to be human in our debates over gay rights."[30] Being human means having the capacity for moral agency and, therefore, making claims on the community, as well as bearing responsibilities.

Reasonable alternatives: At least some marriage traditionalists concede that same-sex couples (as well as unmarried heterosexual couples) might be granted some kind of legal protection. Advocates for same-sex marriage speak more positively that there should be alternatives to marriage, including cohabitation between consenting adults, civil unions, and domestic partnerships. These contractual arrangements offer important rights and protections to unmarried couples and their children. However, they do not provide the social status or the full range of benefits and obligations of marriage. Therefore, most advocates consider them inadequate.

For the most part, advocates agree that legal alternatives to marriage are good, but not good enough to substitute for the "real thing." First, civil unions do not have the immediate name recognition that marriage enjoys. "One of the benefits of marriage is that everyone knows what it is, whether you are at a hospital, or dealing with the government, or explaining yourself in a conversation. Many do not know what a civil union is, and thus civil unions encounter more resistance and are treated differently from marriage."[31]

Second, civil marriage conveys responsibilities and obligations along with rights and benefits. When the legislature in the state of Hawaii passed a measure recognizing same-sex partners only as "reciprocal beneficiaries," it demeaned gay men and lesbians by not fully recognizing them as adult citizens who could bear — and should be expected to bear — certain obligations, as well.

Third, civil unions and domestic partnerships have been purposefully established as parallel institutions to keep gay people permanent outsiders. While these marriage alternatives provide some recognition and protection, they are separate and unequal. Their discriminatory character is especially noticeable when heterosexual couples are allowed legal access to all options, but same-sex couples are granted all options except marriage.[32]

The negative consequences of excluding gays and lesbians from marriage are at least twofold. First, same-sex couples are kept in an inferior position. Second, the institution of marriage is used to legitimate heterosexual superiority. In light of these justice concerns, Robert Williams argues against creating a separate ritual for blessing same-sex unions in religious communities. "Then we would still have *marriage* for some people," he writes, "and something else for others. The implication is that the 'something else' is something *less*. . . . The notion of 'separate but equal' inevitably creates *unequal* institutions."[33] The editors of the *New Republic* argue similarly that the category of civil union is a "pseudo-institution" that works to "erase inequality and at the same time perpetuate it."[34] Not every attempt to modify marriage discrimination, it seems, ends up decreasing oppression against the LBGT community.

Likely consequences: Contrary to predictions of the most dire conse-quences if same-sex couples marry, advocates emphasize the positive consequences if this option is made available. To begin with, the fact that same-sex couples sustain loving, committed relationships under conditions of cultural animosity is nothing less than miraculous. The majority culture could learn from the LGBT community how to "do the work of love,"[35] in J. Michael Clark's phrase, perhaps with greater endurance and flair. Society would also benefit because challenging any form of injustice interrupts prejudice and hate, helps strengthen the well-being of persons, and enhances community. Rethinking the institu-tion of marriage and, in particular, questioning the assumption that mar-riage must be a gendered, hierarchical arrangement would also be gains.

Heterosexual women would benefit because gay marriages will, in Nan Hunter's words, "disrupt both the gendered definition of marriage and the assumption that marriage is a form of socially, if not legally, prescribed hierarchy."[36] To be sure, the rebalancing of power in hetero-sexual relations will not happen automatically because of the legalizing of same-sex marriage, but marriage between two men or between two women has the potential to destabilize the presumed cultural mean-ing of marriage and denaturalize its gendered structure of inequality. Moreover, if heterosexual women had more options for domestic life than marrying men and if they could visualize the possibility of join-ing with another woman to establish a household and raise children, then "their bargaining power within male-female marriage would be greater," and "wives might actually start getting the equal treatment our society has long claimed that they should have."[37] Along these lines, lesbian poet Judy Grahn speaks of her teaching role as an out lesbian in her working-class neighborhood: "Firstly, by my clothes and bearing I model a certain freedom for women. Secondly, as two women living together, my lover and I strengthen the position of every mar-ried woman on the block, whether she knows and appreciates it or not. (Her husband probably does.)"[38]

Children in LBGT households would benefit from living with parents who enjoy rights and protections comparable to those of their heterosexual counterparts. In addition, children growing up to discover their own non-normative sexual identities would benefit from knowing that same-sex relationships are legally sanctioned and societally recognized as valid ways of loving and making a family. Furthermore, children in lesbian and gay-headed families tend to learn that the social world is richly diverse and to develop the personal strength to face the challenges of a sexist and heterosexist society along with poverty, racism, and cultural elitism. When black lesbian-feminist essayist and poet Audre Lorde asked her son Jonathan, then in his early teens, to talk about the advantages and disadvantages of growing up with lesbian parents, "He said the strongest benefit he felt that he had gained was that he knew a lot more about people than most other kids his age that he knew, and that he did not have a lot of the hang-ups that some other boys did about men and women."[39]

Finally, eligibility to marry would benefit LBGT people although advocates do not agree on the precise list of what these benefits would include. As GLAD legal activists put it, "Common sense tells us that if marriage is good for non-gay couples, then it must be good for same-sex couples for all the same reasons."[40] However, to drive this point home to a predominately non-LBGT audience, some marriage advocates have developed problematic assertions. The "marriage as normalizing" argument lifts up the dominant heterosexual culture as normative, identifies successful change as "becoming like them," and downplays any critique of the marital family. Therefore, William Eskridge praises marriage as a prime means for integrating lesbians and gays into mainstream society. "As we shed our outlaw status, we are increasingly integrated into (as opposed to being closeted from) the larger society and its spheres of business, religion, recreation, and education. Recognizing same-sex marriages would contribute to the integration of gay lives and the larger culture, to a nonlegal form of civilizing gays." Marriage would establish common ground between the heterosexual majority culture and the LBGT minoritized culture. "In time," Eskridge proposes, "same-sex marriage will likely contribute to the public acceptability of homosexual relationships."[41]

An even more troubling argument is that marriage will benefit especially gay men because it will have a civilizing effect by reining in uninhibited gay male sexuality. Eskridge makes a legal case for same-sex marriage in a book subtitled *From Sexual Liberty to Civilized Commitment.* Because even in an age of HIV/AIDS gay men have been "more sexually venturesome (more in need of civilizing)," Eskridge proposes that "same-sex marriage could be a particularly useful commitment device for gay and bisexual men."[42] Gay male cruising and experimentation with multiple anonymous sex partners have given way, he contends, "to a more lesbian-like interest in commitment. Since 1981 and probably earlier, gays were civilizing themselves. Part of our self-civilization has been an insistence on the right to marry."[43]

To argue that marriage is a necessary social control mechanism to tame men's sexuality reinforces the sex-negativity that is so much in evidence among marriage traditionalists. To argue, as Eskridge does, that "same-sex marriage civilizes gay men by making them more like lesbians" presumes, falsely, that women are not interested in sex or sexual pleasure but concerned only with intimacy and making relational commitments.[44] Furthermore, is it true that gay men, among others, are in need of "self-civilization" simply because they live and love outside the marriage zone of adult "respectability"? Moreover, when all is said and done, is marriage essentially for the purpose of sexual discipline and control?

Assessing the advocates' case

In promoting justice as equal access, advocates make a compelling case that same-sex couples should be treated no differently from heterosexual couples. Respect for LBGT people requires meeting their basic needs *as LBGT people,* including protecting their intimate partnerships. The marriage debate also shifts the discussion of gay rights from a focus on negative privacy rights (the right to be left alone and free from state interference) to a debate about extending a positive right, namely, recognition of and support for same-sex intimate relationships and families. For this reason, this debate requires a strong *moral* defense of gay rights as human rights.

At the same time, advocates fail, by and large, to provide a moral defense of *gay sexuality,* an omission that puts them at great disadvantage, given the power of compulsory heterosexuality and the pervasive devaluing of homosexuality. Whatever else this marriage debate is about, it is about sex. It is a serious shortcoming for advocates not to provide a sustained critique of the prevailing heterosexist sex/gender paradigm. It is also shortsighted not to raise more directly questions of justice with respect to the institution of marriage itself. In pushing hard for the inclusion of lesbians and gay men (bisexual and transgender persons typically fall by the wayside) within "normal" marriage, advocates have not been interested in asking whether marriage is the right prize. However, the mainstreaming of gay people by gaining access to marriage is a vigorously contested political goal within the LBGT civil rights and liberation movements, not because same-sex partnerships do not warrant recognition and protection, but because marriage is viewed as an oppressive institution.

Because marriage is the culturally designated site for legitimate — that is, both legal and moral — sex, and because non-normative sexualities are routinely stereotyped as dangerous and morally deficient, the topic of same-sex marriage confuses, panics, and deeply troubles cultural conservatives. A ferocious backlash against same-sex marriage has taken place, and in response some within the LBGT community have reverted to a familiar strategy: to seek safety by attempting to normalize homosexuality ("we're just like everyone else"). A major problem with this strategy is that normality is "won" only by *desexualizing* homosexuality and downplaying the very difference that causes the ruckus in the first place.

A gay politics of respectability tries to present homosexuality as an insignificant difference, much like left-handedness or color-blindness. Homosexuality, it suggests, is a private matter without political meanings, only a lifestyle preference. This strategy shifts away from disturbing talk about sex and eroticism and toward more "civilized" discourse about commitment, partnership, and the like.

Legal scholar Martha Minow's analysis of what she calls the dilemma of difference is helpful at this point. In a society in which differences are occasions for domination, stigma, and inequality, the struggle to overcome such inequality is far from simple. "The stigma of difference may be recreated," she observes, "both by ignoring and by focusing on it." While decisions about employment, education, and other benefits, including marriage, should not be based on a person's race, gender, or sexual orientation, it is also true that some groups have more power than others and have constructed the world to grant them privileges while placing others at a disadvantage. Given the realities of power inequalities and social oppression, Minow argues that "the problem of inequality can be exacerbated both by treating members of minority groups the same as members of the majority and by treating the two groups differently."[45]

Marriage traditionalists, operating with an oppositional view of difference, define the difference of gayness as an absolute otherness without redeeming significance. As noted in the previous chapter, Robert Knight is not alone in his judgment that society has no need of gay men and lesbians and, therefore, has no obligation to recognize their intimate partnerships as valid. In this worldview, all differences are ranked hierarchically within a moral dichotomy of good/bad, normal/abnormal, and natural/unnatural. When carried to its logical conclusion, this framework calls for the elimination, not just the exclusion, of the culturally defined inferior other.

Marriage advocates have sought, by and large, to deal with the dilemma of difference by downplaying the difference and emphasizing homosexuality and heterosexuality as morally equivalent. Sex is not addressed head-on, but is rather left tucked discretely behind the "marriage veil" inside a restricted space where few questions need be asked. This strategy is not altogether effective, however, because the cultural majority is not fooled by the privatization of gay sexuality, the efforts to sidestep sex, or the attempts to mute gay identity and culture as a distinctly visible difference.[46]

Without an explicit defense of the goodness of sexuality and, more specifically, of gay sex, the cultural anxieties surrounding homosexuality, same-sex marriage, and even marriage itself will never be properly named. Without being named, they cannot be confronted and worked through constructively. Furthermore, rational argument about same-sex marriage has only limited effectiveness because resistance to full equality for lesbians and gay men is deeply rooted, culturally and psychologically. As Martha Nussbaum points out, "Fear of the erosion of traditional distinctions and boundaries, fear of a type of female sexuality that is unavailable to men, fear of a type of male sexuality that is receptive rather than assertive — all these probably play a role in making the current debate as ugly and irrational as it is." To top it all off, she concludes, "in a such a situation . . . , clarity of argument frequently serves only to intensify the force of opposition."[47]

A strong defense of gay sexuality requires critiquing the notion that the only moral (and legal) sex is heterosexual. It also requires critiquing the notion that the only moral (and legal) sex is marital sex. It is at this juncture that advocates for same-sex marriage falter. In seeking equal access to marriage for same-sex couples, they have chosen, largely for strategic reasons, to downplay criticism of the institution of marriage. They overplay the cultural ideology of marriage as the only legitimate (and legitimating) zone for "good sex." Most troubling, some advocates buy into, or at least draw on, conservative assumptions about the need to keep (gay male) sex under control and about the stabilizing role of marriage in regulating sex. If marriage is, first of all, considered necessary for the social control of women, if the control of gay men is then added on, and if the marital family remains, finally, the only legitimate family, then adding *gay marital* sex into this restrictive sphere of social propriety may be a gain for some, but it will leave unaltered the underlying sexual categories and moral norms which render LBGT people (and others) inferior and at disadvantage.

Playing down sexual difference, recasting LBGT people (or at least lesbians and gay men) as "normal," and sanitizing gay sex are efforts to reduce the threat that gay identity and culture pose to dominant norms. Safety and access to basic rights, including the right to marry, become dependent on making queerness invisible. In the process, the prevailing norms and structures of compulsory heterosexuality are left unchallenged. The moral problem becomes misidentified as the "problem" of homosexuality and whether "they" should be allowed access to "our" (heterosexual) privileges. Defined this way, the solution is for gay people to conform to, or at least not overtly deviate from, heterosexist sex/gender norms and practices.

An alternative, more risky, but in the long term more productive change strategy is to affirm the goodness of gay sexuality, launch a full-blown critique of heterosexist norms and values, and reformulate a sexual ethic that does not presume that everyone is, or should be, heterosexual, married, and committed to procreation. This approach of politicizing sexuality and marriage requires making gay people and gay sexuality *more* public and visible as non-normative identities while, at the same time, doing whatever can be reasonably done to make the world (and church) safer and more welcoming for LBGT people.

In the next chapter, LBGT critics of marriage enter the conversation with a cautionary word and alternative change strategy. The caution is that justice requires more than equal access to a troubled and oppressive institution. The strategy is not to seek marriage rights, but rather to dismantle marriage as a state-sanctioned institution.

CHAPTER FIVE

Marriage Critics

> The question isn't whether
> the state should marry gays,
> but whether it should
> marry anyone.[1]
>
> — ALISA SOLOMON

S AME-SEX MARRIAGE is strenuously debated within, as well as out-side, the LBGT community. In considering whether gay marriage is "a must or a bust," the journal *Out/Look* questions whether the community should make marriage rights a priority. "While few would begrudge any couple the right to publicly celebrate their relationship," the editors observe, "there is less consensus about how much energy we should expend to get the government to sanction those same re-lationships."[2] Others argue that because marriage is a problematic institution with a long and troubled history, LBGT people should not rush to take the plunge. If marriage really is a heterosexual institution and isn't working all that smoothly, why should gay people seek to move onto that turf?

Most marriage critics call for a radical rethinking of sexual, family, and social relations. The full range of diverse human sexu-alities — heterosexuality, homosexuality, bisexuality, transgenderism, intersexuality, and, for that matter, asexuality — should be affirmed and protected. Moreover, as religious studies scholars Janet Jakob-sen and Ann Pellegrini suggest, a more expansive notion of justice and freedom is needed. "We think homosexuals (and their advocates) have been asking for far too little," they write. "Lesbian and gay ad-vocates have been asking for tolerance and equal rights, not freedom and equal justice." What would it mean to "advance the morality of a queer way of life"?[3]

A queer ethic seeks an open, democratic society in which LBGT people among others will have the material conditions and cultural freedom to thrive — really thrive — as respected, contributing members of society. To thrive, people must be free, and freedom in a full sense includes sexual freedom. Such freedom, the capacity to enter into and sustain relations of mutual care, support, and affection, is indispensable to a shared common humanity. Therefore, in the midst of this marriage debate, queer theorists and activists remind all parties that "sexual freedom is not a frivolous question," but rather "a value worth protecting." The freedom to form significant relationships is something that "should not be dismissed as mere self-indulgence, for which it is often mistaken."[4]

Locating the intracommunity agreements and disagreements

While the marriage debate internal to the LBGT community is intense and far from resolved, the intracommunity concerns are different from those that trouble marriage traditionalists and other opponents of same-sex marriage. To begin with, the LBGT community does not get bogged down over the legitimacy of same-sex intimate partnerships or the moral value of homoeroticism. Gayness is affirmed as a good and honorable way to be human. LBGT partnerships and families are embraced in their rich diversity as fully worthy of community support and protection.

In addition, all parties agree that denying same-sex couples the right to marry, civilly and religiously, is discriminatory and unjust, but they arrive at that judgment from different starting points. For example, Claudia Card believes strongly that state regulation of intimate relationships, including marriage, is "probably a very bad idea" and that lesbians and gay men are "better off, all things considered, without the 'option.'" Yet even she does not hesitate to name the exclusion of gay people from the institution of marriage as arbitrary and wrong. "Denying us the option for no good reason," she writes, "conveys that there is something wrong with us, thereby contributing to our public disfigurement and defamation."[5]

Despite their criticism, marriage critics are eager not to allow their disagreements to comfort or abet anti-gay opponents who call the humanity of gay people into question and would severely limit their civil and human rights. For this reason, some queer theorists speak of their awkwardness at being outspokenly critical about something that seems so imminently fair and reasonable, namely, to enlarge the community's options by extending access to a civil and human right. It seems "unfashionable, and perhaps untimely," Michael Warner writes, "[even to question] marriage as a goal of gay politics. One is apt to feel like the unmannerly wedding guest, gossiping about divorce at the rehearsal dinner."[6] However, this whole issue has too many ramifications for the LBGT community not to be addressed fully.

The internal LBGT conflict is not about the status of homosexuality, the desirability of increasing support for alternative families, or even the value of committed intimate partnerships. Disputes have arisen elsewhere, with respect to the institution of marriage, the role of the state in regulating sexual morality, and the goals and interests of the LBGT movement. Isn't marriage such a thoroughly heterosexual (and patriarchal) institution that it is unlikely ever to accommodate gay sexuality and same-sex love? What role, if any, should the state play in regulating intimate life? Is it not the case that state regulation unavoidably establishes hierarchical distinctions between "good" and "bad" sexualities, "good" and "bad" families, and rewards the good while punishing the bad? If so, shouldn't marriage as a state-sanctioned institution be abolished or at least have its status reduced? Finally, where's the wisdom in focusing the LBGT community's limited energy and resources on acquiring the legal right to marry? Shouldn't gay politics be committed to a broader, more comprehensive justice agenda and give priority to larger concerns?

This questioning underscores how differently LBGT people, as cultural outsiders, approach the marriage issue in comparison to their heterosexual counterparts. When a (white, middle-class) heterosexual couple ponders marriage, they have the freedom — no, the luxury — to pose the question exclusively in personal terms, asking whether *this* person is the right partner or whether it is better to marry now or later.

While weighing their choices, heterosexual couples are able to take for granted that theirs is a congenial and supportive cultural context in which to make their decision. The power of the state authorizes them to make these highly personal, life-defining decisions as a matter of course. Moreover, the state is ready and willing to extend to them the status of "legally married" and bestow an array of rights and responsibilities, all for the asking.

In contrast, for heterosexual couples that elect not to marry, things are far different. They experience not-so-subtle state coercion *to* marry by the mere fact that so many social and economic benefits are withheld from them if they cohabit but do not marry. Pressure, including strong cultural expectations, only increases should they have children.

For lesbian and gay couples, matters are even more constraining. In most places it is not safe for same-sex couples even to hold hands in public, much less turn to the state for licensing their intimate partnerships. Marriage is not a gay-friendly institution, but rather the linchpin that holds heterosexual privilege in place and stigmatizes gay love and gay sexuality as morally unacceptable and out of bounds. Given this context of marginalization and state persecution, the LBGT community must ask whether marriage as an institution is worth entering. In a negative cultural context in which the state, through its sodomy laws, has long prosecuted gay people as criminals, those within the LBGT community cannot even begin to address the more personal kinds of questions without first wrestling with the politics of marriage and sexual oppression.

This chapter examines how marriage critics make their case against same-sex marriage while confronting anti-gay oppression and supporting the struggle for sexual justice.[7] After reviewing their arguments against marriage, this chapter offers an assessment of the LBGT marriage critics' case in light of a progressive Christian ethical commitment to gender and sexual justice.

The deficits of marriage

Marriage critics agree that as long as heterosexual couples are free to marry, then same-sex couples should have the same rights and responsibilities. However, they insist that a narrow focus on gaining the right to marry fails to reflect the wider, more transformative social agenda of the LBGT movement. Acquiring marriage eligibility would not address problems that matter much more to most gay people, including access to health care, HIV prevention, job discrimination, the repeal of sodomy laws, anti-gay violence, media coverage, and the ordinariness of the heterosexist presumption that "straight is good, gay is bad."[8] At the same time, there are benefits in at least asking the marriage question. For one, more people have become aware of the heterosexism of marriage and of the discriminatory nature of current marriage policies. Even the mainstream proposal to push for marriage rights advances the cause of equality and helps validate gay lives and relationships.[9]

Even so, marriage critics continue to question the advisability of endorsing marriage, given the problems with the institution of marriage and the injustice of a social system that legitimates only a singular form of intimacy and family relations, the marital family. "As long as lesbian and gay people have a choice," theologian Mary Hunt writes, "I urge us to take leadership in breaking the two-by-two pattern that is alleged to have begun with Noah and his nameless wife." Rather than reinforce compulsory coupling, the notion that a person is incomplete unless bonded for life with another ("opposite sex") person, the Christian tradition should identify as its central relational norm "not coupledness, but friendship." Friendship between both sexual and nonsexual partners is open to various relational possibilities beyond the confining pair bond of husband and wife. Marriage as one option is fine as far as it goes, but in Hunt's judgment, "the heterosexual marriage norm is inadequate to the needs of most people and should be replaced by friendship."[10]

Other marriage critics raise similar objections. Legal activist Paula Ettelbrick's essay "Since When Is Marriage a Path to Liberation?" identifies concerns that have been reiterated and amplified by others in the intracommunity debate. First, marriage has historically been a patriarchal institution, reflecting and reinforcing men's ownership of women, children, and property. Such an institution perpetuates gender injustice and women's inequality. Second, marriage is the prime "bearer of the heterosexist norm," granting legitimacy only to heterosexual intimate relationships and turning those who are unmarried and sexually active into moral suspects and, literally, criminals. Furthermore, marriage establishes a "hierarchy of normalcy," rewarding those who most closely approximate procreative, marital heterosexuality and stigmatizing those who deviate from the norm, most visibly out gay people who speak openly and positively about their "wayward" sexual desire. Third, the institutionalizing of heterosexuality through marriage upholds the conventional nuclear family as the exclusive norm for personal life and denies the validity and contributions of LBGT and other nonmarital families.[11]

While the search for affirmation and legal protection is understandable on the part of same-sex couples, given the cultural vilification of nonheterosexuality and the equation of adult status (and citizenship) with heterosexual monogamy, critics warn that acquiring the right to marry will not be liberating. On the one hand, marriage will require gay people to deemphasize their difference from the cultural majority and present themselves as "just like everyone else." The price of acceptance will be to submerge their gayness and render gay sexuality invisible, so as not to rock the boat or cause discomfort. Ettelbrick cautions, "Marriage will not liberate us *as lesbians and gay men*. In fact, it will constrain us, make us more invisible, force our assimilation into the mainstream, and undermine the goals of gay liberation."[12] On the other hand, extending marriage rights to gays will not likely have a transforming effect on society. Such a move will do nothing to challenge a social system that values marriage above other relationships. In fact, a new division will be created between "good gays" who marry and "bad gays" who do not.

Other marriage critics agree that marriage should be critiqued as a political institution that reinforces heteronormativity and pressures people into compliance. Should marriage become available to same-sex couples, they will face not only a new option, but also new pressures. In writing about her own intimate partnership with another woman, Claudia Card speaks about the compulsory character of marriage: "Still, we are not married. Nor do we yearn to marry. Yet if marrying became an option that would legitimate behavior otherwise illegitimate and make available to us social securities that will no doubt become even more important to us as we age, we and many others like us might be pushed into marriage. Marrying under such conditions is not a totally free choice."[13]

Card and others link marriage to four "unfreedoms," constraints that marriage places on personal freedom. First, many people's economic security is tied to marital status whether because of social security, health insurance, immigration law, or tax benefits. Women often find themselves pressured to enter into marriage in order to survive financially. Second, and a continuation of the benefits problem, many people remain in loveless, even destructive marriages because divorce is difficult to attain or not a realistic option, given their economic vulnerability. Again, women suffer more than most men because of their relative powerlessness. Third, marriage is based on monogamy, and yet many people "have more than one long-term intimate relationship during the same time period." The marriage model is, therefore, limiting and does not reflect the different ways in which couples structure their partnerships. Fourth, marriage grants partners legal access "to each other's persons, property, and lives" that "makes it all but impossible for a spouse to defend herself (or himself), or to be protected against torture, rape, battery, stalking, mayhem, or murder by the other spouse."[14] For many women, marriage is one of the least safe places, and same-sex married couples would not be spared those difficulties. In light of these problems, Card asks, "Why, then, would anyone marry?"[15]

In response to that question, some marriage critics suggest that the best argument they can muster in support of same-sex marriage is that gay people might transform the institution by disrupting the prevailing cultural assumption that marriage, in order to work properly, requires a gender hierarchy of male authority and female dependence. However, as discussed in the previous chapter, marriage advocates, in their zeal to gain the cultural majority's support for marriage rights, have adopted a rhetorical strategy that downplays the transformative potential of gays entering marriage. Furthermore, they publicly accept rather than challenge how heterosexual marriage is currently practiced.

To underscore marriage as an unjust institution, Nancy Polikoff challenges the conclusions some marriage advocates draw from historical and cross-cultural research about a wide range of same-sex unions, including Native American berdache traditions and early Christian rites celebrating fraternal partnerships. William Eskridge has drawn on this history, for example, to argue against the assertion that marriage has always been an exclusively heterosexual institution. But in her examination of these historically diverse patterns, Polikoff calls attention to something else. Few if any of these same-sex relationships, even those which Eskridge terms marriages, depart from the patriarchal paradigm of a two-gendered, hierarchically ordered marriage. "Although both partners were biologically of the same sex," Polikoff writes, "one partner tended to assume the characteristics and responsibilities of the opposite gender, with both partners then acting out their traditional gender roles." Her question is this: "Will lesbian and gay marriage 'dismantle the legal structure of gender in every marriage,' or does this research instead suggest that the gendered nature of marriage, and indeed of all society, will survive same-sex unions?"[16]

The freedom of outsiders

Marriage critics argue against embracing the flawed institution of marriage. In their judgment, the LBGT community would do better to direct its energies toward creating its own traditions and alternative partnership and family patterns. In contrast to marriage advocates who regard exclusion from marriage as a serious deprivation, marriage critics regard their status as "marriage outsiders" differently. Residing on the margins means freedom to critique the status quo and also entertain new ways to create family systems.

If queers, that is, nonconformists who dissent from the socially approved patterns of gender and social relating, are recognized and respected as valued members of the community (as opposed to being forced to deny their sexual identity and/or practice in order to "become respectable"), then the reigning hierarchies of "good" and "bad," "normal" and "abnormal" sexualities must be reexamined. The customary categories for describing and making sense of human sexual diversity can no longer be taken for granted as adequate. The practice of ranking differences as morally superior or inferior is called into question, as well as the marital family that grants privileges and status to the heterosexually married, but disenfranchises and devalues all others.

To be sure, marriage critics are not interested in idealizing cultural marginality, but they see advantages in living and loving outside the marriage system. As Alisa Solomon puts it, "Banished from the privileges of marriage, we've been spared its imperatives."[17] Not subject to the procreative heterosexual norm or pressured into compliance with predetermined gender and family roles, same-sex couples have a precious freedom — and unregulated space — to experiment with interpersonal relationships and family forms. Because sex is freed from the presumption of only heterosexual meanings, same-sex couples "exalt our love in and for itself" without having to seek justification beyond the delight of giving and receiving mutually desired pleasure. Mutually shared pleasure is its own reward and a powerful means for building intimacy between persons. At the same time, the freedom of outsiders from heteronormativity is a demanding freedom, requiring people to be reflective about their choices rather than accepting of the predetermined forms and roles that are expected of most heterosexual couples.

Research on same-sex couples illustrates their inventiveness in creating alternative family patterns and so speaks of nonconformity as a source of insight. "In coming out, nonheterosexuals choose to reject the heterosexual assumption," the prevailing notion that heterosexuality alone is valued and valuable. "In so doing," Jeffrey Weeks observes, they "become involved in creating new knowledge of how it is possible to be in the world."[18] While the dominant heterosexual culture encourages strongly gendered family roles for men and women and plays up differences in power and status, in contrast same-sex couples place greater emphasis on an egalitarian relational ideal. This queer commitment, queer because it is deliberately oppositional to heterosexist norms and patterns, calls for ongoing negotiating of roles and responsibilities on a more equitable basis.

A second feature of many same-sex intimate partnerships is an emphasis on the couple's community connections. The focus is not on a supposedly autonomous, self-sufficient couple in isolation, but rather on how two people, both as a couple and as individuals, contribute to and are supported by an extended network that includes friends, ex-lovers, biological family members, and the larger community. This extended network, not just the "free-standing" couple, is recognized and celebrated.

Critiquing the politics of sex

The struggle, as marriage critics define it, is how to gain the legal rights and protections necessary for safeguarding LBGT people without surrendering what is at the core of queer life and queer love, namely the freedom both to be different and act differently. Standing apart from heterosexual culture because of a separation both imposed and elected, gay people have the freedom to create something different: more egalitarian, democratic intimate relationships. Marriage does not appeal to these critics because they fear that entering into marriage will mean assimilation into the dominant culture. The "normalization" of queers will result in cooptation and a loss of freedom, including their dissenting voice. If gay people buy into such a powerfully "normalizing" institution as state-sanctioned marriage, critics fear that the queer community will lose its hard-won visibility as an alternative culture organized around sexual difference.

Marriage advocates, in turn, seek to allay these fears of cooptation by insisting that marriage will not be forced on LBGT people. Rather, same-sex couples will be given, as a matter of personal choice, the opportunity, at last, to decide for themselves whether to marry or not. E. J. Graff writes, "No one will force same-sex couples to darken the institution's doors: we'll merely gain the choices available to heterosexual pairs."[19] However, this invocation of personal choice is deceptive, marriage critics warn, because civil marriage always involves a third party in addition to the couple: the state with its considerable powers not only to grant privileges and material benefits, but also to enforce its notion of sexual morality and order. As Michael Warner argues, "Sexual license is everything the state does not license, and therefore everything the state allows itself to punish or regulate. The gay and lesbian movement was built to challenge this regulatory system."[20]

As long as the state authorizes only some relationships (sexual affiliations in the form of heterosexual marriage) through its licensing and regulatory powers, it will use its power to define some people and relationships legitimate and others illegitimate. On this score, marriage critics are clear that state-sanctioned marriage is not neutral or apolitical. Instead, marriage is a key component of a total social system that reinforces other unequal power relations, including political and economic arrangements. Moreover, through the regulation of marriage, the state enforces a certain notion of morality. In the United States, as discussed in chapter 1, the reigning marriage model is a Protestant Christian paradigm of lifelong, monogamous heterosexual relationships with a provider-husband and nurturer-wife, preferably at home caring for their dependent children. "In the realm of sex," Janet Jakobsen and Ann Pellegrini write, "we have a *de facto* established sexuality, heterosexuality. This is why there is a 'coming out' day only for homosexuals. (Every day, it seems, is heterosexual day....) In the United States, heterosexuality is also a *de jure* established sexuality. Heterosexuality is privileged in federal and state laws, from immigration to taxation to healthcare."[21]

Tolerance of difference, including sexual difference, is preferable, of course, to hostility, overt hatred, and anti-gay violence, but tolerance is also a limited response to injustice and oppression. Insofar as tolerance maintains the underlying schema of a normative insider and non-normative outsider, difference will be framed in terms of superiority and inferiority. In a tolerant society, LBGT people might be accepted as different, but the foundational inequality persists, all to the detriment of those defined as non-normative. As Weeks points out, "Cultures are perfectly able to accept the idea that some people are different without fundamentally shifting their values or power structures."[22]

A state-sponsored marriage system not only distributes material benefits to some and withholds them from others; it also dispenses cultural legitimation by authorizing some relationships but not others. Through the institution of marriage, the state upholds the "heterosexual assumption" that singles out heterosexual relating as the exclusively good and decently ordered pattern. At the same time it invalidates all nonheterosexual activity. This dynamic helps account for the fierce resistance to extending marriage rights to same-sex couples. Although the cultural majority might well come to regard same-sex marriage as at least partial conformity by LBGT people to heteronormalcy, thus far it has not worked that way. In a culture of inequality in which dignity and status depend on superior/inferior rankings, the heterosexual majority has chosen to hold on to marriage as the prime signifier of its superiority. "They want marriage to remain a privilege," Warner writes, "a mark that they are special. Often they are willing to grant all (or nearly all) the benefits of marriage to gay people, as long as they don't have to give up the word 'marriage.' They need some token, however magical, of superiority."[23] What marriage critics find so troubling is that gay people who seek marriage rights are, consciously or not, playing into this elitist, anti-democratic game. As Warner queries about gay and lesbian "marrieds," "Would they not in turn derive their sense of pride from the invidious and shaming distinction between the married and the unmarried?"[24]

To break the monopoly control of marriage, LBGT critics propose two strategies. First, they urge the disconnecting of marriage from the wide range of legal rights and economic benefits that the state currently distributes on the basis of marital status and instead to make those benefits, including social security and health care, available to all residents of the community. If basic rights were guaranteed regardless of marital status, people would be less likely to marry solely or primarily for reasons of economic security. They would also be less likely to stay within unsatisfactory partnerships. Individual freedom, as well as personal dignity and well-being, would be enhanced.

Second, the state should cease licensing any particular family or partnership form and thereby disestablish the marital family as the singular state-sanctioned associational pattern. The state should instead be neutral toward the diverse family and intimacy patterns through which people meet their relational needs. Disestablishment of marriage would also mean the disestablishment of heterosexuality as the normative sexuality. The state would no longer (need to) regulate sexual relations between consenting adults. The one exception, as Jakobsen and Pellegrini argue, are those "cases that are otherwise of concern to the state, like those of violence and abuse. Importantly, what makes, or should make, rape and other forms of sexual violence actionable is not their connection to sex or sexuality, but their enactment of violence and abridgment of consent."[25]

If marriage were no longer privileged and regulated by the power of the state, then a couple's decision to marry (or not) would be determined on other grounds, most likely on the basis of their desire to have their covenant witnessed and celebrated by their community, including their faith community if they were connected to a religious tradition. By removing itself from the marriage business, the state would no longer regulate intimate life. However, it would have another, more constructive role to play: guaranteeing that all community members have access to the material conditions they need for a decent life, including health care, employment, adequate housing, personal safety, and so forth. In other words, the state would retain a positive role, according to at least some LBGT marriage critics, in providing "the necessary prerequisites for freedom, including the freedom to form intimate relations of our own choosing."[26] This right of self-determination with respect to making intimate connections is crucial for personal freedom and moral self-direction. Therefore, Claudia Card speaks for many marriage critics when she states, "I would rather see the state *deregulate* heterosexual marriage than see it begin to regulate same-sex marriage."[27]

Beyond individual rights

While a centrist gay rights movement has focused on acquiring civil rights and legal protections for LBGT people, a diverse and left-leaning queer liberation movement has insisted on a social vision and change agenda much broader than the expansion of individual freedoms. The goal of liberation struggle is not merely to attain equal rights for individuals, as important as these are, but also to encourage social transformation, including the renewal of religious and cultural traditions, so that the world may become safe and welcoming of sexual and other kinds of difference.

A queer perspective on justice calls for resistance to oppression in all its complex varieties. Sexual and other differences should not be occasions for domination, but rather promoted as complex variations within a richly diverse common humanity. It also calls for the self-affirmation of LBGT people, but not in isolation from other marginalized groups. A LBGT liberation agenda fosters the dignity of all persons and seeks collaboration with others to make the political, economic, and cultural conditions available that will allow all people to lead decent, meaningful lives and participate openly in shaping communal life together. If social change becomes reduced to seeking gains only for one's own group apart from the justice struggles of others, then solidarity across lines of social difference is broken and authentic community is not possible.

In keeping with this liberation perspective, marriage critics speak of the limitations of a rights-based approach to social change. Nan Hunter writes, "The political viability of rights-based movements depends on an acceptance — and thus strengthening — of the existing system, which in turn preserves patterns of dominance by some social groups over others."[28] Similarly, pushing for inclusion in the marriage system typically means that gay people must soften, if not abandon, their critique of the institution of marriage because it is not possible to publicly critique the institution of marriage and "simultaneously ask to be let into it."[29] A pure "rights" analysis also fails, Paula Ettelbrick argues, to incorporate a broader understanding of the underlying inequities that operate to deny justice to a fuller range of people and groups. Thus, attaining the right to marry may extend benefits to some gay and lesbian couples electing to marry, but it will leave unaltered the legal and cultural discrimination against gay, lesbian, and straight people electing not to marry. "Thus," Ettelbrick concludes, "justice would not be gained."[30]

A queer notion of justice looks beyond gaining marital benefits for some to the reordering of social power and the rebuilding of community. In a time of significant economic turmoil and social conflict, the religious and political Right has organized by pitching to people's fears and resentments, thereby blocking redistribution of political and economic power. Calls from women, people of color, and LBGT people for extending civil and human rights are fiercely resisted and discredited as "selfish appeals" to supposedly special rights. In response, the LBGT community and others have organized to become more politically visible, but the effort by some to win public approval by "mainstreaming" gay people has required playing down the difference of gayness. The queer movement is de-queered and presented as if it were entirely white, middle-class, and family-oriented. As a result, two things have happened. First, the effort to gain acceptance on the dominant culture's terms has deepened divisions within the LBGT community between a politics of inclusion and a politics of resistance. Second, the rights-based movement has become focused on acquiring other state-sanctioned rights and privileges, including the right to enlist for military service as out gay people. For queer activists and theorists, all this signals an abandonment of a more radical cultural critique.

Marriage critics point out that the effort to acquire marriage rights has been spearheaded, to a great extent, by lawyers and other professionals within the LBGT community who already possess considerable social privilege. For them, gaining access to marriage would be another step toward their full inclusion in and acceptance by a social order they embrace as theirs, but it will not necessarily ease the load for those doubly or triply harmed by gender, race, and class injustice. By and large, few gay men have incorporated into their pro-marriage arguments a feminist analysis of marriage and its limitations. Similarly, white-skinned marriage proponents have typically failed to integrate a class and race analysis into their "equal rights" framework. In addition, marriage advocates have tended to oversell marriage as a solution to a range of social problems. For example, same-sex marriage is touted as a way that medically uninsured gay people can take advantage of a working partner's health care benefits, but marriage advocates have not put comparable effort into addressing the more pressing crisis for many within the LBGT community and elsewhere: the absence of decent jobs with adequate benefits, the paucity of job training programs, and the geographic as well as economic barriers to affordable health care, including health care for people living with HIV/AIDS.

Marriage critics identify another problem with attempting to gain equal rights by mainstreaming or "normalizing" LBGT people. By presenting gays as "like everyone else," advocates for inclusion minimize the difference that gayness has to offer the culture. Queer sexuality becomes invisible and displaced, left literally without space within the cultural imagination. For this reason, marriage critics are adamant that the right to marry will not necessarily increase respect for gayness or gay sexuality. Gay sexuality would likely become submerged within the very institution that has singularly devalued gayness as a willful (or at least unfortunate) departure from heterosexual norms and practices. If gay sexuality were to become gay *marital* sexuality, it might well receive protection from the state and even toleration from the wider community, but only in spite of its gayness. It would perhaps gain relative legitimacy, but only because it would be marital and, therefore, protected by the marital privacy screen.

Dismantling the heterosexist difference paradigm

The battle to be fought is not narrowly over marriage rights, but about dismantling a heterosexist difference paradigm that devalues gayness and refuses to acknowledge the moral equivalence of gay and non-gay sexuality, of gay and non-gay love. According to heterosexist norms, expressed in official Roman Catholic moral theology and other religious traditions, what is objectionable is not (necessarily) *being* gay but rather *acting* gay, *loving* gay, and *affirming* gayness as a morally sound and legitimate part of human diversity.[31]

A narrow focus on marriage rights leaves prevailing heterosexist (and sexist) cultural norms unchallenged. In the dominant sex/gender paradigm, what determines a person's psychological and moral fitness is whether he or she is erotically attracted to the right gendered ("opposite-sex") person, as well as to the "right" race, class, religion, and so forth. This construction of sexuality defines morally legitimate sex as male-dominant heterosexual sex within marriage. Such sexuality is considered well ordered because of clearly differentiated gender roles of reproduction and childrearing. The "gay difference" is defined in terms of nonreproductive sexuality, fluid gender roles, "free" sex (that is, sex outside of marriage), and deviant sexual desire. What makes sexual desire deviant is not so much that it is same-sex. After all, the status quo can tolerate closeted sex between two men or two women if they are discrete and do not openly challenge heteronormativity or the sanctity of marriage. Rather, dangerous sexuality is "out," gay-positive, and queer sexuality that is politically vocal and personally "esteemed" in its desire for human connections that refuse to reinscribe male gender supremacy or order erotic life hierarchically.

The queer community dissents from the dominant culture's notion of dignity based on inequalities of rank. It affirms instead a common dignity for all persons based on the shared desire to love and be loved and to make meaningful, intimate affiliations in and through the body or, better yet, in and through diverse, sexually empowered bodies. As Michael Warner explains, "The point of a movement is to bring about a time when the loathing for queer sex, or gender variance, will no longer distort people's lives."[32]

The threat posed by LBGT liberation is its potential for destabilizing compulsory heterosexuality by making visible an attractive alternative for organizing intimacy and erotic desire. Because gay sex is nonreproductive, the sex desired is entered into and justified only by the intimacy it enhances. Once sex is released from a procreative imperative, and once gay people become visible in everyday life, then sexuality can no longer be summarily contained within the confines of male-dominant, female-subordinate marriage. The danger posed by a visible, nonapologetic gay sexuality, Michael Bronski suggests, "is not that heterosexuals will be tempted to engage in homosexual *sexual* activity (although the visibility of such activity presents that option), but that they will be drawn to more flexible norms that gay people, excluded from social structures created by heterosexuality, have created for their own lives."[33]

Marriage critics argue that by standing nonapologetically outside the normative structures of reproductive heterosexuality and male-dominant marriage, gay people are witnesses to, and representatives of, an alternative way of being erotically empowered. Same-sex lovers come together not on the basis of duty or conformity to external rules and societal expectations, but rather freely, on the basis of mutually desired intimacy. However, to say "freely" is not entirely accurate because gay people must resist their oppression and stand in opposition to dominant cultural norms in order to make space for their lives and loves as gay people. Standing in moral defiance to sexual injustice is risky in a sex-phobic, moralistic, and punitive culture that presumes that sexual identity and practice define personhood. Such defiance has also sparked alternative moral wisdom. As Mary Hunt writes, "We have much to teach: our strong reliance on one another for survival, not simply on our partner, if we have one, but on our community; life with dignity and fun even if we are not partnered; endless variety in how we make our lives work in the face of oppression. These are valuable contributions that, when taken seriously, will reshape the ethical norms of our [Western] society."[34]

Marriage dissidents argue against relying on the state to license (and thereby legitimate) intimate partnerships. Marriage should not be the exclusive signifier of family. Instead, society should follow the lead of the LBGT community and define partnerships and families functionally, as diverse and intentional networks of people who are committed to each other's well-being and form intimate partnerships not by an action of the state, a religious ceremony, or even blood ties, but because of desire. Against tremendous odds, people have listened to, and taken seriously, their "forbidden longings" to bond for the purpose of sharing pleasure, loving mutual care, and daily support. Some of these bonded relationships are sexual, but not all. Social space and support should be extended, as well, to nonsexual, intimate partnerships and friendships for people who choose to live communally as family. The marital family does not exhaust the options for either making family or making love.

Assessing the marriage critics' contributions to this debate

Marriage critics are helpful in reminding other parties to this debate about justice in relation to diverse human sexualities. Current social policy is based on the exclusive (and excluding) marital family model that is no longer relevant to how considerable numbers of people, gay and non-gay alike, live their lives. In urging more creative thinking about marriage, intimate partnership, and family making, marriage critics insist on a greater openness to sexual pluralism and learning from those on the margins about reordering personal life in more democratic, egalitarian directions. What is happening culturally is not "a thinning of family commitments and responsibilities, but a reorganization of them in new circumstances."[35]

Marriage critics make other contributions to the same-sex marriage debate by demonstrating the following:

- a strong desire to protect, nurture, and celebrate human difference, including diverse human sexualities;
- a commitment to an egalitarian ideal for personal and social life with an emphasis on flexibility, negotiation, and mutuality;
- a determination that gender roles and expectations for men and women alike be investigated and critiqued, along with assumptions about race and class;
- a disgust with the conventional, historically patriarchal model of marriage as a hierarchical power relationship based on ownership and control;

- a dissatisfaction with the centrality given to "the couple" and an investment in the power of friendship networks for rebuilding community; and

- an insistence that basic economic and social benefits customarily attached to marriage should be made available to all persons regardless of their marital status.

Perhaps their most important contribution, however, is keeping the focus in this marriage debate on social justice rather than on individual rights alone.

What might be said about the three specific concerns that marriage critics bring to this debate: marriage as a flawed institution, the role of the state in legitimating marital heterosexuality (and repressing other options), and whether the LBGT movement should seek inclusion in or a radical transformation of dominant cultural practices?

Is marriage transformable?

About marriage, there is little question that this social institution has a troubled history. At the same time, at least some marriage critics run the risk of essentializing marriage as fixed and unalterable. A more complex judgment is called for, recognizing marriage as flawed but changeable. Rather than speaking of *the* institution of marriage, it is better to speak in the plural of a diversity of *marriages* in order to differentiate egalitarian, justice-centered marriage from other contenders.

About the transformability of marriage, marriage critics come across as overly pessimistic about possibilities for change. Nan Hunter advocates the right to marry for same-sex couples, but she is not sanguine about the prospects of altering social power relations between men and women. Nonetheless, she believes that same-sex marriage has at least some potential "to disrupt both the gendered definition of marriage and the assumption that marriage is a form of socially, if not legally, prescribed hierarchy."[36] That potential is worth exploring even though marriage by itself is no panacea. In fact, no single strategy or institutional change will alter entrenched patterns of heterosexism and sexism, any more than dropping the legal barriers thirty-five years ago against interracial marriage ended white racial supremacy.

Marriage inclusion may be a step, even a large step, toward sexual justice, but it is by no means the final or only one that matters. One problem is that rights-based campaigns tend to oversell the gains that may actually be made. In addition, focusing on gaining equal access tends to reinforce, not challenge, the status quo. That said, it is also true that incremental, rights-based changes may serve as "incubators, modifiers and regenerators of demands for far-reaching change."[37] When journalist Anne Quindlen quips, "Gay marriage is a radical notion for straight people and a conservative notion for gay ones," she takes into account that marriage, on the whole, remains a more conservative gesture.[38] Even so, marriage advocate Evan Wolfson suggests that marriage could well be "conservatively subversive," given that marriage is so highly prized in this culture and yet there is still such widespread resistance to recognizing lesbian and gay couples as "marriage material."

To argue that gay people should have a right to marry does not mean that they must accept the institution as given. An institution may be deeply flawed, but that by itself is not a sufficiently compelling argument against participating in it. If that were true, the only appropriate change strategy would be to abandon all institutions with which people are currently affiliated. Rather than abandon marriage, the movement to extend marriage rights to same-sex couples is an opportunity to redefine that institution from the inside.[39] Although nothing can be guaranteed in advance, their wager is that change is possible through the collective moral agency of LBGT people working in concert with their allies.

Consider yet another response to the objection that marriage is intrinsically problematic and should be shunned. Access to the material benefits of marriage is very important to some, if not most, same-sex couples. Gaining those benefits alone may justify seeking to change marriage policy. Beyond this, marriage has symbolic value, offering recognition that a couple has a relationship important and valuable enough for them to be perceived as "next of kin." Marriage is certainly not the only means for establishing close ties, but it is a widely acknowledged avenue by which lesbians and gay men could gain further visibility as partners and family.

Achieving that increased visibility and social standing as "marriage peers" might truly be transformative. "Until current sentiments in our society are changed," Christine Pierce suggests, "lesbians and gay men will not be able to expect that ethical (and legal) principles will be applied fairly to them. Thus, it is important for the sake of creating new sentiments to press for gay marriage."[40] Altering sentiments will, of course, not guarantee sexual justice. However, with respect to jurists and policy makers who consistently fail to recognize same-sex relationships as legitimate family commitments, it would be a positive step to see LBGT people marry and no longer be regarded as "unattached" individuals or strangers before the law, but rather as the loving partners and beloved kin they are.[41]

Does the regulatory state have a positive role?

About the role of the state in regulating sexuality and personal life, queer theorist Michael Warner is adamant that the state's intrusion into these matters is entirely negative. The common cultural presumption, he notes, is that "controlling the sex of others, far from being unethical, is where morality begins." Through marriage policies, sodomy laws, and other mechanisms, the state imposes on everyone a single, state-regulated sexual morality. By legitimating only the marital family, the state is in effect embracing "one identity or set of [sexual practices and] tastes as though they were universally shared, or should be."[42] To correct this problem, he argues that the state should adopt a hands-off approach when it comes to sexual expression and allow adults the free exercise of sexual autonomy.

Warner's critique of a moralistic, pro-marriage state politics is well placed. His concern is also appropriately directed toward protecting the sexual freedom of consenting adults from restrictive legal prohibitions. In a pluralistic society where there are multiple conflicting notions of the good, including the sexual good, it is not appropriate for the state to legitimate only one (rather narrow) definition of human sexuality and family relations and penalize others as deficient or detrimental to the common good. To the contrary, a liberal society should make room for sexual and other differences.

The state should be willing to intervene in matters of sexuality and intimacy in order to protect vulnerable parties, especially children, from exploitation and harm and, further, to adjudicate conflicts when these arise, as, for example, when local communities struggle with how to regulate pornography and at the same time protect free-speech rights.[43] However, the role of the state should not be to impose a single moral standard or enforce of set of uniform expectations on adults. As Martha Nussbaum argues, there is a positive, quite legitimate role of the state "to encourage, not to stifle, innovations and deviations in living, in order to discover the most fruitful ways to realize its ideal of human dignity."[44]

Marriage critics are helpful in their critique of a state-sanctioned politics of sexual control, in their call to limit the state's regulatory power, and in their insistence about protecting the freedom of sexual minorities. Where they are less helpful is in not conceding that the state may also play a positive role in protecting people's freedom, including their sexual autonomy. Some laws, such as sexual harassment laws, interfere with supposedly "consensual" relationships of co-workers, but in a sexist culture in which men have been socialized to regard women as sexual property, anti-harassment laws are needed to *constrain* certain activities and thereby *protect* the sexual autonomy of others, in particular the sexual freedom and bodily integrity of women. Contrary to the warning that state regulation is anti-freedom, at least some state regulation functions to enhance rather than compromise (some) people's freedom. "A simple 'get the state off our backs' position may look attractive when we are thinking about the sex lives of middle-class men," Nussbaum writes, "but it is clearly inadequate to deal with the situation of women and other vulnerable groups. There is no consent where there is pervasive intimidation and hierarchy."[45]

In keeping with their objections about state regulation of sexuality, marriage critics are inclined to see sexual ethics as another mode of control aimed at rewarding conformists to heterosexist norms and punishing nonconformists. Again, Warner speaks for many when he contends that queer politics must "resist any attempt to make the norms of straight culture the standards by which queer life should be measured."[46] The merits of this stance are, first, its challenge to double standards and, second, its implicit call for rethinking ethical guidelines about sex, intimate relationships, family, and social relations more broadly. The downside is that marriage critics so emphasize sexual freedom that they tend to communicate a minimalist ethic based exclusively on consent.

Consent is an indispensable component of any ethic that takes mutual respect and care seriously. Furthermore, consent is a fundamental commitment to be honored in all sexual relating. However, consent has been invoked at times as if it gives permission for sexual license. In this instance "free consent" favors the powerful and disadvantages the vulnerable. "Because the community's primary concern has been to defend 'unrestricted sexual freedom,'" J. Michael Clark laments, "we have evinced no concern for the power dynamics or the social and medical consequences of our so called consensual sex; our consent has carried with it no sense of accountability."[47] On the one hand, marriage critics are right to critique a moralistic politics of compulsory heterosexuality and state-sanctioned marriage. On the other hand, because they have not sufficiently clarified the difference between sexual freedom and sexual license, they run the risk of an "anything goes" ethic.

Are resistance and accommodation mutually exclusive?

About the goals of the LBGT movement, marriage critics regard the quest for marriage rights as a sign of cooptation by the dominant culture, the equivalent of going after mainstream "respectability." This comes at the cost of submerging, if not losing altogether, the distinctiveness of queer identity, queer culture, and a queer cultural critique. However, is it necessary to set up an either/or choice between accommodation and resistance?

Many LBGT activists and "ordinary rank and file" members rely on a rather complex social change model that values both movements: the pull of outsiders to criticize and challenge, and the push of insiders to gain inclusion and construct new possibilities. "The language of 'family' used by many contemporary non-heterosexual people can be seen," Jeffrey Weeks and associates write, "as both a challenge to conventional definitions, and an attempt to broaden these; as a hankering for legitimacy and an attempt to build something new; as an identification with existing patterns, and a more or less conscious effort to subvert them."[48]

Similarly, ethnographic studies of lesbian and gay covenanting ceremonies show how same-sex couples, in publicly ritualizing their intimate partnerships, are engaging both in resistance, by defying the prevailing anti-gay cultural definitions of their lives, and in social conformity, by participating in ceremonies of commitment that for all appearances replicate wedding services. Ellen Lewin argues that the rituals same-sex couples have devised to "marry" simultaneously challenge and reinforce tradition, "suggesting that efforts to distinguish between resistance and accommodation may be less meaningful than many theorists have assumed."[49] In keeping with this viewpoint, it is not when gay people press, but rather when they *give up*, their claim on marriage (and other institutions) that they most conform to the dominant culture's rules and expectations. Accordingly, seeking the legal (and religious) right to marry may not be at all assimilationist, but rather a confrontational challenge to the heterosexist marriage monopoly that refuses to acknowledge the human dignity and rights of nonheterosexual people.[50] From this perspective, same-sex marriage may even be described as a form of civil disobedience.[51]

Where marriage critics are most persuasive is when they insist that the pursuit of marriage, if it is to be pursued at all, must be grounded in, and accountable to, social justice and the dismantling of structures of privilege and exploitation whether based on gender, race, class, or

sexuality. Continually, the question must be asked of marriage advocates: how would acquiring the right to marry further the cause of
justice, understood as a comprehensive call to transform oppression
of every kind? How does "getting married" give rise to resistance to
injustice?

The next chapter turns to consider whether and how a contested
Christian tradition might contribute to the fostering of a genuine
passion for justice.

CHAPTER SIX

Contested Christian Teaching

> *I think it useful to acknowledge*
> *that Christianity has relatively*
> *little wisdom on sexuality.*[1]
>
> — MARY E. HUNT

ANY EFFORT TO renew moral and religious tradition with respect to sexual difference and intimacy is ambitious, perhaps
even foolhardy, given how marriage exclusivism is widely presumed
to be simply the "way things are." Making movement forward will
require critical and constructive moments. The critical moment requires honestly investigating Christianity's sex-negativity, including its
denigration at times of even heterosexual procreative sex. The constructive moment involves articulating an ethic that celebrates not
only heterosexuality, not only married sexuality, and not only procreative sexuality, but human sexuality in its diverse, morally principled
expressions.

Because sexuality, this remarkable human capacity to make connections with others, is intrinsic to our humanness, promoting sexual
well-being is a way to strengthen the human good. Moreover, it can
spark a wonderfully "wild desire" for justice as rightly related community. It matters greatly, therefore, whether a particular ethic or
religious tradition fosters an "ethic of desire" that stimulates people to
move toward justice or further entraps them in injustice. The agenda
in this chapter is to consider how Christians might promote a desire
for sexual justice by examining what Christians should, and should no
longer, teach about sexuality, marriage, and intimacy.

The power to critique and rebuild

Despite their differences, marriage advocates and critics concur that changing marriage policy will require sustained struggle. Even then, a favorable outcome is far from certain. The passage in recent years of federal and state DOMAs (Defense of Marriage acts) indicates the kind of fierce resistance that can quickly mount to prevent welcoming same-sex couples as marriage equals. To date, only a few religious traditions have authorized the blessing of same-sex unions.

While it is true that LBGT people belong to every social group and faith tradition, on their own they lack sufficient power to alter societal structures and transform religious and moral norms. However, what lies within their grasp is exercising what Elizabeth Janeway calls the "powers of the weak." These powers are, first, the power to critique, dissent from, and delegitimate alienating cultural norms, and, second, the power to enter into alliances with others to promote a more inclusive justice.[2] Happily, some of the staunchest allies in the quest for sexual justice are non-gays.[3]

The good news is that the numbers of heterosexual allies are on the increase.[4] Countless heterosexual women and men have come to register within themselves, and often publicly express, their own dissatisfaction with the sexual status quo, including the marital status quo. They, too, yearn for a reliable alternative. The high divorce rate and decline of the two-parent, wife-at-home family are signs that the prevailing family ideology no longer matches the lived reality of even the cultural majority. Other seismic cultural changes include the feminist movement's challenge to male power and authority, the efforts across the board to enhance the status of women and children, and the ongoing scrutiny given to gender roles and gender parity.

Of particular significance is the decoupling of sex from procreation. Contracepted rather than procreative sex has become normative for most heterosexual couples, most of the time. This cultural shift alone has had profound impact on people's lives, especially the lives of sexually active heterosexual women whose fear of unintended (and problem) pregnancies has been diminished because of the availability of effective contraceptives and of medically safe, legal, and affordable abortion as backup. When heterosexual sex is no longer driven by the procreative imperative, both men and women are more likely to focus on sexual pleasure as a way to enhance intimacy, what theologians describe as the unitive purpose of sexuality.

Although LBGT marriage critics worry that the current push to acquire marriage rights reflects how (some) gay people seek to mimic heterosexuals, it can be argued, to the contrary, that something far more interesting and potentially transformative is under way. To a considerable extent, the majority heterosexual culture is coming to resemble gay culture with its "notorious" gender flexibility, its openness to and experimentation with diverse family forms, and its "indulgence" with respect to the pleasures of nonprocreative sex. "Contrary to popular belief, and even some gay rights rhetoric," Michael Bronski writes, "gay people have not been patterning their lives on the structures of heterosexuality; rather, the opposite has occurred. Heterosexuals who have increasingly been rejecting traditional structures of sexuality and gender have been reorganizing in ways pioneered by gay men and lesbians." This process may be thought of as *reverse assimilation*. The lesson in all this, Bronski adds, may be that "only when those in the dominant culture realize that *they* are better off acting like gay people will the world change and be a better, safer, and more pleasurable place for everyone."[5]

The fear of sex

The transformation of intimate life in this direction — toward becoming "a better, safer, and more pleasurable place for everyone" — requires coming to terms, positively, not only with the difference represented by the lives and loves of LBGT people, but also with the power and place of sexuality within the culture. In the popular mind, gayness is associated with "free" or unrestricted sexuality (that is, undisciplined and uncontrolled sex because it is nonmarital and nonprocreative). The disparagement of gayness, often expressed as a "fear

of flaunting," communicates disapproval of an explicitly positive eroticism. While gay people may be more or less tolerated, gay sexuality
is not. Because of this, safety for gay people has often been attained
by "passing" as if not gay, that is, as heterosexual and "under control"
in a way that "out of control" gay people cannot be. In other words,
while it may be okay to "be gay," it is not okay to "do gay."

This status/conduct distinction appears in legal and theological discourse, especially when believers are admonished to "love the sinner
but hate the sin."[6] Erotophobia, or "fear of flaunting," is pervasive in
a society that is, at one and the same time, both fascinated with and
repelled by sex. "Our culture manages to be both pervasively prurient
and puritanical, tolerant and judgmental," William Eskridge notes.
"Same-sex couples can often, though not always, live middle-class
lives in small towns. The trade-off is that the couples are expected
not to flaunt their sexuality."[7]

The problem here is not that a minoritized group exists or has become increasingly visible, or even that this subculture regards erotic
pleasure as a life-enhancing resource. The trouble arises from the
dominant culture's alienation from the body, sexuality, and the erotic.
Heterosexual dis-ease with things sexual has been projected onto gays
who have, in turn, become the cultural carriers for the majority's un-
resolved fears and anxieties, as well as its unfulfilled desires, including
the longing to integrate sexuality more fully into its notion of the
human person and of the human community. Rather than welcoming sexual difference and living at ease with the erotic, the dominant
heterosexual culture has constructed its norms and sensibilities on the
basis of a restrictive, punitive sexual paradigm that is heterosexist and
makes male-dominant heterosexual coupling compulsory.

Sexual fundamentalism is the notion that there is one and only one
ideal sexuality — heterosexual, marital, and procreative. Those abiding by this standard are given permission, even the duty, to police
others and keep them under regulatory control. Although variation,
diversity, and pluralism are characteristic of all of life, somehow "sexuality is supposed to conform to a single standard. One of the most
tenacious ideas about sex is that there is one best way to do it, and

that everyone should do it that way."[8] This sexual code may also be termed "marriage exclusivism" insofar as the only legitimate way to be sexual in the culture is as a "respectfully" married person, licensed by the state and living with a partner through "benefit of clergy."

Making progress toward sexual justice, including the public recognition and protection of same-sex partnerships and families, requires an inclusive ethic that debunks sexual fundamentalism, draws larger parameters than the conventional marriage ethic, and incorporates at a deep level appreciation for benign sexual variation. A progressive ethic appreciates the goodness of erotic pleasure and its bonding power and, therefore, approaches it with care and thoughtful consideration, but not with fear or shameful loathing. However, precisely because of the cultural, and specifically religious, hegemony of heterosexual marriage, it is challenging to envision a truly progressive ethic that would honor a diversity of sexual identities and the many ways in which people live responsibly as sexual persons, outside as well as inside marriage.

Such a progressive ethic is not for the purpose of controlling or constraining sexual desire, contrary to the concerns of queer theorists who object to the regulatory character of state-sanctioned marriage for gays or anyone else. Rather, its purpose is to *empower* people so that they may live more freely in their bodies, deepen their capacity for and enjoyment of tender, erotically charged lovemaking, and make truly life-giving decisions about both their giving and their receiving of intimate touch. Broadly speaking, decisions are life-giving that demonstrate concrete respect for both self and other, thereby encouraging relational well-being.

Sexual oppression as patriarchal Christianity's enduring legacy

What would Christians say about same-sex marriage if their interpretive lens reflected a commitment to sexual justice as one aspect of a more comprehensive social justice? Granted, this may not be the most likely scenario, given that the Christian moral legacy about sexuality has been, with very few exceptions, fear-driven, punitive, and controlling — in short, oppressive. Moreover, at this moment Christian churches are deeply divided over sexual ethics and especially the morality of homosexuality.

Patriarchal Christianity, by elevating spirit over body and male over female, has shown little interest in reversing the sex-negativity that runs throughout the history of the Western church. When it comes to sex, the Christian tradition reflects a lingering suspicion about the body and "carnal pleasures." Even the slightest hint of eroticism can set off alarms, especially when exhibited by the unmarried young or by "the old," whether married or not. Theologically, Christians declare that God's creation is worthy to be pronounced good and emphasize God's dwelling en-fleshed in the midst of life. However, in the popular mind, Christianity is associated with discomfort with respect to actual (sweating, aging, imperfect, differently abled, and variously colored and gendered) bodies, with fear of women's social and reproductive power, with disrespect for LBGT people, and with a reluctance to validate pleasure as a moral good, even among the properly married. Given Christianity's sex-negativity and abiding influence in shaping cultural sensibilities, theologian Carter Heyward contends for good reason that "*sexual* justice [may be] the most trivialized, feared, and postponed dimension of social justice in western society and, possibly, in the world."[9]

Jewish theologian Judith Plaskow's description of her own tradition's ambivalence about sexuality is reminiscent, as well, of similar Christian theological responses. (To be truthful, Christian leaders, particularly male celibate clerical elites, have expressed far more negativity than ambivalence about these matters.[10]) From the vantage point of patriarchal Judaism and, I would add, patriarchal Christianity, eroticism has been viewed as an ambivalent power, granted a certain place in life because it serves the good end of procreation, but held at arm's length because it also threatens to overwhelm and do harm unless constrained. Because patriarchal religion associates women with the power to tempt men toward sin and sensuous excess, men have sought to keep themselves safe from "women's wiles." The institution of male-dominant marriage has provided the "safe container" into which fathers could (literally) hand their daughters over to husbands, who thereby gained the right to control her, albeit benignly and lovingly, "for her own good" and, apparently, for his. Property rights have been equally central to marriage, especially the transmission of (male) property through inheritance by only "legitimate" heirs.

Insofar as sex has been viewed as a threatening power and marriage as the container for this unsettling energy, it makes sense that both Jewish and Christian traditions would share a similar understanding that the "problem of sexuality" (and patriarchal traditions perennially cast sexuality as a *problem*) is that of assuring male control of women's lives, their sensuality, body labor, and reproductive powers. In keeping with this legacy of ownership and possessiveness, dominant Christianity's response to sexuality has been fearful and reactive, preoccupied more with the prerogatives of the powerful than with the suffering of the powerless. The watchwords have been control and discipline, but mastery has seldom meant men's *self*-discipline. More typically, it has meant male entitlement to exert mastery over others and the created order. Therefore, when it comes to sexuality and gender power, Christianity's project has been thoroughly political: to keep men in charge of women, less powerful men, children, and the earth, all of which are culturally associated with body and sensuality (rather than mind, rationality, and spirituality).[11]

Given how this arrangement is celebrated as the natural order of creation, the constructive project of imagining sexuality *without* patriarchal controls and free of sexism and heterosexism becomes difficult. As religious feminists have long insisted, the social control of women has shaped basic attitudes and sensibilities about sexuality, the body, marriage, and family.[12] Without male control of sexuality and women, supposedly all hell would break loose. In the patriarchal imagination, marriage is absolutely necessary as the bedrock institution that undergirds (propertied men's) civilization. Should the day ever arrive when male-dominant marriage no longer serves as the foundational control mechanism, what could possibly keep the world upright, much less make sex safe and children morally legitimate?

The specter of same-sex marriage is this: it threatens to disassemble the carefully contrived structure of compulsory heterosexuality and its denial of homoeroticism. Could it be, as the Christian Right fears, that once the erotic genie is let out of the bottle, nothing would effectively stand in the way of rampant hedonism, sexual permissiveness, and total moral chaos? Are gay people really that powerful to threaten the breakdown of the marital family and of civilization itself?

Counteracting such fears will, at the very least, require putting securely into place something that Christianity has not yet managed to produce: a genuinely "good sex" ethic based on gender equality and nondominative power relations. In that context, good sex would mean sex that is both erotically powerful and ethically principled. These criteria should inform a Christian "good marriage" ethic, as well. Before proceeding to that discussion, however, it is wise to note something of a bittersweet irony. The sweetness is that many contemporary Christians (and others) gladly promote an understanding of marriage as an intimate partnership between two equals who promise in good faith to share their lives and fortunes, including the joys of sexual intimacy. The bitterness is that in espousing such egalitarian partnerships, they, too, must stand in *discontinuity* with the bulk of Christian tradition. For centuries, Christian marriage has been anything but a partnership between equals or an "approved" site for erotic enjoyment.

Marriage as controller of sex and women

Ours is a culture in which it is difficult to talk openly about sex, largely because sexual mores have been so thoroughly influenced by Christian sex-negativity. Celebrating the power and goodness of human desire, taking passionate delight in one's body and in other people's bodies, and reveling in the giving and receiving of sensuous pleasure: none of that sounds very Christian, does it? For many, Christianity is synonymous with prohibitions against sex. Under the influence of Christianity, as Gayle Rubin quips, sex is "presumed guilty until proven innocent."[13]

Given the pervasiveness of Christian sex-negativity, historian Mark Jordan offers some candid advice for those who would consider sexuality from a Christian perspective: "Listening for long to some supposedly 'Christian' discourses about sex," he writes, "can confuse clear thinking and dull moral sensibility. So hearers have good reason to be suspicious at the start of [any] speech about Christian ethics."[14] After examining biblical views of sex, Jordan goes on to survey theological perspectives from ancient, medieval, and reformed sources. Only then does he reach his conclusion: "They speak not instruction or encouragement for better sex; they speak warning or prohibition against sexual pleasure. We read lists of sexual sins and cautions against the power of sexual excess."[15] What is not found, he observes, is "advice [even] to married couples on how to have more pleasurable sex.... There is no Christian 'pillow talk' or *Kama Sutra,* no Christian saints are revered for attaining the vision of God through disciplined erotic refinement."[16] At this point, you can almost see him throw up his hands as he asks, "What is it about Christianity and sex anyway?"[17]

Nothing clarifies the oppressive character of the conventional Christian sex/marriage construct more than a close reading of early Christian and Reformation texts. When Christian theologians reflected on sexuality at all, they promoted either perpetual virginity (or chastity, meaning no sex) or a marriage ethic that focused on sexual (and social) control. However, making room for sex even within marriage has been a contested issue among Christian moralists. For the longest time within the history of the church, good sex was defined as "no sex," that is as sexual abstinence and voluntary celibacy. Because of the deep suspicion that sexual pleasure tends to excess and threatens to overwhelm reason, early theologians carved out only a narrowly defined space for sex within the confines of tightly regulated marriage. Although Christians were permitted to have sex, the purpose of sex was limited to procreation. There was no justification given for the pursuit of pleasure between intimates. Such desire was unthinkable, and dire warnings were given about temptations toward sin even within marriage.

When Augustine addresses the question of the marriage good, he argues, somewhat generously, that marriage is not intrinsically sinful. Husband and wife may, indeed, enjoy a special bond, but at the same time they are admonished to exercise restraint, keeping in mind that even marital sex is tainted by sin and that celibacy is the preferred state. The better wisdom was that "married couples should strive to limit intercourse to what is necessary for procreation and look forward to an early cessation of sexual activity by mutual consent."[18] Many theologians assumed — or perhaps hoped — that marriage partners would grow "beyond sex," once the heat of youthful lust had dissipated. (Recall the discussion above about the cultural discomfort with — and actually disgust may not be too strong a word — for the sexually active older person, even if married.)

These ancient theological perspectives are certainly at odds with modern sensibilities that celebrate marriage, elevate it as a sign of entry into adulthood, and make it nearly compulsory for men and women if they wish to be in good standing in church and society. However, throughout most of Christian history, marriage has been thought a second-rate choice. "At no point does Augustine," for example, "concede that marriage is for Christians a choice equal to the choice of life without sex."[19] Yes, sex may be permitted to Christian husband and wife, but even then, marriage is no license for sexual pleasure or erotic freedom. Quite to the contrary, marriage is a guarded space within which to contain, restrict, and subject sex to careful controls. Therefore, Christian theologians not only restricted sex *to* marriage, they also restricted the kind of sex they considered legitimate *within* marriage. "In many ways," Mark Jordan argues, "the theology of Christian marriage has been the effort to promote sex without eroticism."[20]

With the Protestant Reformation, some reevaluation of marriage and family life occurs, but even then, the church fails to develop anything close to a comprehensive ethic of sexuality. The celibacy/ marriage dichotomy is upended. Marriage is elevated as the higher calling for Christian disciples, not so much because marriage is seen as better spiritually or morally, but because the Reformers were alert to the power of sinful lust and had strong doubts that a consistent lifestyle of celibacy was attainable. Marital sex is permitted because it can serve the good ends of procreation and companionship, but even these are qualified or "hedged" goods. Sinful lust continues to be a serious problem among even the married.

While the Reformers elevate marriage over celibacy, they also promulgate a restrictive marriage ethic in which good sex remains exclusively marital and procreative. Pleasure is dangerous. Therefore, Protestantism carries forward the Augustinian tradition and, like Roman Catholicism, has in many respects been overdetermined by the elder Augustine's linkage of sex with sin. Luther and other Reformers believe that "all *should* marry," Rosemary Ruether points out, "because God's intention from the beginning had been to unite men and women in marital union and bid them to procreate." However, they also insist that "almost all *must* marry because the sinful urges that had arisen from the Fall could be contained without sin only in marriage."[21] Marriage, Luther said, is a "hospital for sinners," a community-sanctioned institution for taming and controlling sex. Within marriage, "fallen man" might redirect his lustful sexual energy toward the legitimate goal of making babies with his wife.

In the Christian tradition, sex is confined and restricted sex. Christian sex is also *patriarchal* sex. Male-dominant marriage is the one site in which sex is granted legitimacy. Within this marital zone, husband and wife may be partners and even spiritual equals, but, nonetheless, the man remains in charge. While the Protestant notion of companionate marriage is widely celebrated, the fact remains that "the companionship of husband and wife was never that of equals." Marriage was "assumed to work harmoniously only when the wife understood herself as an obedient subordinate and the husband as a beneficent but authoritative patriarch."[22] In the dominant theological tradition, marriage remains a gendered structure that normalizes inequalities of power, status, and role between the partners and makes sex "respectable" only because it keeps it tucked away and under wraps.

Marriage as exclusive norm

Marriage exclusivism insists that procreative marriage is the only legitimating norm for sex. Accordingly, all sexual activity is judged
in relation to marriage. Although Augustine and the Protestant Reformers remained suspicious even of marital sex, most contemporary
Christians depart from tradition by assuming that sexual activity in
the context of heterosexual marriage is good and appropriate. However, in blessing marriage, Christian moralists have given little or no
attention to domestic violence, marital rape, or spousal neglect. (It has
been the feminist movement in religion that first brought sustained
attention to these matters by recasting them not as sexual sins, but as
ethical violations of power and role, including the problem of clergy
betrayal of trust.[23]) At the same time, considerable attention, almost
all negative, has been given to pleasure and its dangers. We must look
long and hard to find Christian theologians making any kind of substantive case for the moral goodness of erotic pleasure. We must look
even longer and harder to find interest in women's sexual pleasure
or erotic empowerment. (Again, religious feminists and LBGT activists and scholars are the ones who have engaged in groundbreaking
ministry and theological reflection on these issues.[24])

If the sex in question is *premarital,* it is questionable but for the
most part tolerated if the couple intends to marry (or at least does not
publicly express their opposition to marriage). Recently, Bishop John
Spong and William Countryman in the United States and Adrian
Thatcher in the U.K. have recommended that the church reclaim the
custom of betrothal to make room for at least some nonmarital sex.
Spong sees betrothal less as a "trial marriage" and more as a period
in which a man and a woman are entering into a committed (yet not
legally formalized) relationship, are finding their way to marriage, and
may, therefore, be permitted sexual intimacy.[25]

Taking a different tack, Thatcher suggests that a "biblical understanding of marriage *assumes* the practice of betrothal"[26] and then
contends that "alongside the near-universal assumption that marriage
begins with a wedding, [there] is another, equally traditional view

that the entry into marriage is a process involving stages." Historical perspective about these matters can be helpful. In the eighteenth century, about half of all brides in England and North America were pregnant at their weddings. Citing the work of historian Lawrence Stone, Thatcher argues that the customary practice has been to begin sex "at the moment of engagement, and marriage in church came later, often triggered by the pregnancy."[27] He concludes that today, "Hundreds of thousands of couples who [are] in defiance of the churches' official teaching [that sex should be postponed until marriage] are reminding us in the churches that they are sharing part of the Christian tradition after all."[28]

If the question is about *extramarital* sex, the assessment is that this is bad, especially if it is the wife who strays. If it is the husband and he is discrete, a double standard typically protects male prerogatives. After all, an androcentric presumption holds that men are more sexual than women and, therefore, need extra outlets. Even Thomas Aquinas argued that prostitution might be tolerated as a necessary evil, permitted by God in order to prevent sinful male lust from erupting and causing greater improprieties. "Sewers," Aquinas writes, "are necessary to guarantee the wholesomeness of palaces."[29] In other words, prostitution is a means to protect "good" wives from the lustful, immoral demands of their husbands, and yet "married ladies" are hardly exempt from succumbing to the dangers of sexuality. As Rita Brock points out, "Prostitutes supposedly exhibited the sexual licentiousness inherent in all women, which good women repressed."[30] According to this view, marriage serves a useful societal function by restraining both women and men and minimizing the temptation toward immorality. However, the truly "holy" elected a different path altogether: celibacy and a life beyond sex.

Finally, if the sex in question is between two men or two women, such eroticism meets none of the criteria for Christian authorized sex. In fact, Christian warrants are difficult to come by for endorsing sex for the purpose of pleasure, either with or without a partner. (Think of the proscriptions against masturbation and, as recently as the late nineteenth and early twentieth centuries, the moral purity campaigns in

North America dedicated to wiping out the "solitary vice.") Moreover, because patriarchal Christianity thinks of sex only within the context of (male-female) social domination, it has not provided adequate guidance for integrating sex and love, especially insofar as Christian sex does not require either social equality or mutual respect. For patriarchal Christianity, sex (and love) is viewed in terms of power and control. The traditional Christian vocabulary shows little evidence of, or interest in, an egalitarian notion of sex as mutually desired intimacy or of erotic touch between equal partners. In many respects, therefore, the culture has been out ahead of Christian and most other religious traditions when it comes to moral wisdom about sexuality.

According to Christian marriage exclusivism, gay men and lesbians are "out of control" because they reside outside the marriage zone. As displaced persons, LBGT people (and others) have had to invent alternative ways of creating family and community that are transparently more flexible about gender roles, less rigid about sex, and more committed to power sharing. Standing on the margins (or being pushed there) has given gay people a measure of freedom from compulsory heterosexuality. Because such freedom might become "contagious," the religious Right has launched a "traditional family values" campaign to depict life outside of marriage as difficult, dangerous, and tragic in order to dissuade the heterosexual majority from thinking that such freedom might be desirable. Accordingly, the so-called gay lifestyle is caricatured as crassly sexual, chaotic, and disease-prone in order to underscore its inclination toward excess and premature death. The anti-democratic Right, using the "hot button" issues of sexuality and race to arouse and manipulate its following, fears freedom as genuine body-respect and bodily/communal self-determination and instead celebrates duty as obedience and conformity to external authority. Gay sex and "welfare queens" are the Right's favored icons of all that threatens "Christian (read: patriarchal and Euro-American dominated) civilization."

In Christianized culture, if gayness is code language for immaturity, sexual promiscuity, and a generalized immorality, then the marital family is held up as the contrast. For this reason, the religious Right can scarcely imagine that same-sex marriage could be anything other than an oxymoron. Respectable people are those who make a serious (marriage) commitment, willingly restrain their sexuality, and settle down, thereby establishing their credentials as properly heterosexual. Patriarchal Christianity's responsible, heterosexually married adult also happens to be the preferred member of most congregations.[31]

In designating heterosexual marriage as the exclusive site for legitimate sex, the church has locked together two oppressive dynamics. Compulsory coupling reinforces the notion that a person is incomplete and deficient unless complemented by his or her "other half."[32] As noted earlier, the pressure to couple is so strong in North American culture that the vast majority of adults marry during their lifetime, and some do so multiple times. Prior to the sixteenth century, Christian tradition had made room for alternative modes of discipleship, including the single, unattached believer and those living within monastic community. Within Protestantism, those options have given way entirely to marriage as the exclusive Christian pattern for right living.

The second dynamic, compulsory heterosexuality, places social pressure on all persons to conform to prescribed gender roles that normalize power and status inequalities. Male-dominant/female-subordinate heterosexuality has been naturalized as the operative norm for social and sexual interaction. Eroticized sexism is expected to be life-long, in sickness and in health, for richer or poorer.

The call for an ethical eroticism

The conventional approach to Christian sexual ethics is so irredeemably flawed that it begs for reconstruction, not piecemeal reform.[33] Religious teachings have been based on fear of the body and estrangement from sexuality. The notion of virtue promulgated has been dependent on repressing bodily feelings, devaluing women, and disrespecting lesbians and gay men. (For the most part, bisexual and transgender persons have not warranted enough consideration even to elicit critique or condemnation, something of a mixed blessing.)

Why is patriarchal Christianity's legacy about sex and marriage in-adequate? Perhaps the most direct answer is because it is constructed on the basis of gender and sexual oppression. Injustice is intrinsic to a binary gender paradigm that defines difference oppositionally, elevates body over spirit, male over female, and heterosexuality over homosexuality, and, furthermore, presumes that right order re-quires a superior party to control its inferior, albeit "complementary" counterpart.

This Christian sexual paradigm has had negative consequences for many, causing inestimable suffering by fostering alienation from the body and the earth.[34] An incarnational faith tradition has been dis-torted into a moralistic, abusive system of control that has used shame, guilt, and violence to keep people in line. For many people, Christian-ity and other patriarchal religious traditions have offered not life but death. Therefore, the trustworthiness of religious traditions and their moral authority depend, to a very great extent, upon their radical reformation through the healing of the body/spirit, female/male, and homosexual/heterosexual dualisms. As liberation theologians have long recognized, spiritual vitality depends on doing justice and seeking a rightly related *bios* or alternative way of life.

For progressive people of faith and good will, the task can never be to transmit an inherited moral or religious tradition uncritically, but rather to engage in open-ended ethical discernment in order to cri-tique teachings and patterns of practice as needed, as well as transform the tradition in more life-enhancing directions. In the effort to con-front a patriarchal tradition shaped largely by celibate male clergy, new conversation partners are radically altering religious discourse about sexuality, a development that greatly troubles marriage traditionalists. Women and LBGT people, including women and LBGT people of color, singles, people who have divorced or never partnered, survivors of sexual abuse, younger and older persons, people living with disabil-ities, and many others are posing new questions, contributing fresh insights, and encouraging a paradigm shift toward an egalitarian ethic of erotic delight, bodily integrity, and the empowerment of the disen-franchised.[35] Very different watchwords apply to this reconstructed

Christian ethic of intimacy: not fear, ownership, and control, but rather responsible freedom, respect for difference, and commitment to end exploitation and the abuse of power.

Reconstructed approaches to sexuality, informed by feminist and LBGT perspectives and in accord with the best scientific insights about human development and social interaction, posit a different notion of sexuality than appears in most traditional Christian theological works. Understood positively, sexuality refers not only to genital sexual activity, but also more broadly to the basic human capacity for relationship and intimacy through embodied touch and deep communication. Without our sexualities, we would be human, but not recognizably so because sexuality touches so powerfully on spirituality, as well as physicality.[36]

A clear indicator of the need for a revised sexual ethic is the increasing gap between conventional Christian moral teachings and how most people live their lives. Certainly one explanation often forwarded for this gap, particularly by social conservatives, is that "sin abounds," but it is not very likely that this generation of people has become flagrantly more irresponsible than any previous generation. Rather, the gap is widening primarily because the inherited moral code is woefully inadequate. As discussed earlier, traditionally, only two options have been available, celibacy and lifelong heterosexual marriage, but that convention no longer stands uncontested. Many people recognize other options as valid even if not officially authorized. Countless numbers of single adults, among them older people in retirement, are sexually active and living together "without benefit of clergy." Many are active Christians who regard themselves fully capable of making responsible choices about how to live and love. For their part, many LBGT people maintain healthy, morally responsible intimate relationships, also without ecclesiastical or legal sanction. Finally, there is increased awareness that not everything within the bounds of heterosexual marriage is morally acceptable, given high rates of domestic abuse, marital rape, and partner abandonment.

The conventional sex ethic — celibacy for singles, sex only in marriage — is no longer adequate, if it ever was, for two reasons. First, the Christian marriage ethic has not been sufficiently discerning of the varieties of responsible sexuality. Second, it has not been sufficiently discriminating in naming the ethical violations of persons even within marriage. A reframing of Christian ethics is, therefore, needed that realistically addresses the diversity of human sexualities while placing the focus not on the "sin of sex," but on the use and misuse of power and how to enhance the dignity of persons.

A single standard: Justice-love

Christian ethical concern should be grounded in an open-ended commitment to actualize three interrelated components of sexual justice: an affirmation of the goodness of sexuality and embodiment, a genuine honoring of sexual difference and respect for sexual minorities, and a willingness to attend to both the personal and political dimensions of sexual injustice and oppression.[37]

An alternative ethical framework is grounded in at least these six values: (1) the goodness of bodies and pleasure; (2) body right, or the principle of bodily self-determination; (3) mutual respect and consent; (4) fidelity as a commitment to honesty and fairness and an ongoing willingness to renegotiate the relationship to serve the needs of both parties; (5) taking responsibility to maintain wellness while avoiding disease and unintended pregnancy; and (6) a willingness to explore the justice implications of sexuality for persons and their communities. Ethically principled sex insists on freedom from control, manipulation, and exploitation, but it does not rest there. People should be empowered to claim the goodness of their own bodies and equipped to understand and direct their use. At the same time, each person has a responsibility to respect the bodily integrity and self-direction of others.

In sum, the central expectation — and single standard — for relationships should be *justice-love,* understood as mutual respect and care and a fair sharing of power. Because I am persuaded that justice-love should replace procreative heterosexual marriage as the guiding norm for intimacy, I am also convinced that a renewal of Christian ethics about sexuality and intimacy requires at least four things.

First, marriage should be decentered. While it is true that marriage is one place in which people may live responsibly as sexual persons, it is not the only place. Therefore, it is appropriate not to privilege marriage as the exclusive or ideal mode of human intimacy. At the same time, we should advocate only egalitarian options for structuring intimate relationships, including egalitarian marriages. Friendship, as feminist and queer theorists suggest, is the most enduring basis on which to construct relationships of mutual respect, care, and abiding affection.[38]

Second, a plurality of benign sexualities should be affirmed. At the same time, plenty of recognition should be given to how doing marriage or any other long-term partnership decently requires maturity and relational savvy on the part of its participants, as well as community support and, above all, fair economic policies.

Third, mutual pleasure should be seen as a morally worthy pursuit within intimate relationships. The guiding moral interest should no longer be to discourage sex or even to promote marriage, but rather to equip people with the skills and insight they will need to assess and improve the quality of their intimate (and other) relationships. The goal is to become more informed, responsible, and passionate justice-lovers by learning what gives each other pleasure and joy. That moral knowledge will surely include awareness that pleasure can also stir an unquenchable desire to contribute to a more ethical world.

Fourth, sex also should be decentered as the defining criterion for partnerships, marriage, and families of any sort. The marital family is one way to establish networks of care and intimacy, but by no means the only or necessarily the best way.

Reversals in Christian moral teaching

The renewal of Christian teaching about sexuality and marriage requires the critique of a morally deficient religious past, but more is needed. A reclamation of core values and commitments from Christian tradition is also called for, most especially an abiding commitment to justice-love. When interpreted through the experiential lens of the LBGT community and its allies, that commitment may yet prove able to offer ethically sound guidance and encouragement.

In urging the development of a justice-centered Christian moral discourse about sexuality and intimacy, I am making a wager similar to the one that ethicist Larry Rasmussen makes in another context, namely, that Christianity can help, but not without reformation.[39] Although Christian tradition conveys a strong sex-negativity with a moralistic bent toward control, the good news is that this tradition is neither monolithic nor unchanging. On a broad range of concerns from family values to divorce and from abortion to gay rights, there are voices of critique and dissent in addition to those calling for compliance and opposition to change. As a living faith tradition, Christianity along with other religions must either adapt to changing conditions and altered awareness of the human condition or risk becoming irrelevant, increasingly decadent, and merely reactionary.[40]

Dramatic shifts in Christian teaching have already occurred with regard to women's status within marriage, their leadership in church and society, and the need for gender-inclusive liturgical and theological language. Similar changes have been accomplished or are well underway with regard to contraception, assisted reproductive technologies, abortion, and the status and rights of LBGT people. Theologian John Cobb illustrates the dramatic character of such changes by examining shifts in attitude among Protestant Christians in terms of divorce and remarriage. "Protestants are becoming so accustomed to this acceptance of divorce and remarriage as the best response in many circumstances," Cobb points out, "that they might forget how drastic a change this is from past Christian teaching." Since Protestants often rely on biblical guidance to resolve moral issues, the change regarding divorce is "particularly noteworthy since it is the acceptance of a practice that is rejected explicitly in the Bible." In fact, Cobb underscores, "It is Jesus himself who opposed divorce!"[41] The fact that a reversal on divorce has taken place is strong proof of how a religious tradition can remain vibrant by staying open to change and revision.[42]

What has propelled Protestant Christians to rethink contraception, divorce, and other issues? First and foremost has been a persistent call, typically from those not well served by the status quo, to set wrongs right and relieve suffering that has been compounded by rigidly applied religious pronouncements. Interestingly, these reversals have rarely been embraced as radical departures from tradition. Instead, they are usually justified as efforts to retrieve the tradition's own best insights that somehow have been neglected, misunderstood, or misapplied. Many Protestants prefer to think, for example, that they have chosen to alter their viewpoints on specifically biblical grounds after critiquing interpretations that distort the Bible's true message. Others highlight this entire change process as the movement of the Spirit calling forth prophets and critics who call the community to repentance and renewal. Whatever the grounds for shifting sentiments and convictions, as Cobb concludes, the point is that if Christians are prepared to reverse positions on such matters as contraception, divorce, and remarriage, they should also be open to reconsidering other traditional teaching, including the topic of marriage "for heterosexuals only."[43]

Biblical scholar Elisabeth Schüssler Fiorenza argues, similarly, that while all traditions within a pluralistic and contested Christianity should be *taught*, because believers need to be knowledgeable about, and come to terms with, both the moral highs and lows of their history, not every tradition should be *preached* and declared truthful as life-giving "good news."[44] All religious claims must, therefore, be subject to moral scrutiny and evaluation according to the most considered moral wisdom of the day. As argued in chapter 2, a preference should be given to the critical readings and constructive proposals that emerge "from below," from those who resist their oppression and are joined in the justice struggle by an assortment of allies. In this process of moral critique and reenvisioning, a vision of a more inclusive human (and cosmic) good may well be grasped. If so, then the historian's take on this process of adaptation and reinvention of Christian moral insight becomes all the more helpful: "One benefit of remembering old church controversies," Mark Jordan writes, "is to be reminded how many of them have been surpassed."[45]

The current marriage debate offers the Christian faith community yet another opportunity to repent of its sex-negativity, sexism, and heterosexism. Christians have been notorious in their reluctance to celebrate how God has created a variety of sexualities, and they have expressed far too little respect for, much less real delight about, that rich diversity. The fact of the matter is that some are heterosexual, others are gay, lesbian, bisexual, transgender, or transsexual, and still others are asexual. All the while, each deserves to love and be loved gracefully, compassionately.

This controversy about marriage, sexuality, and family also gives Christians (and no doubt others) an opportunity to embrace some good news about sexuality and sexual difference. As argued in this chapter, the primary norm should no longer be marriage, hetero-sexuality, or procreative possibility, but rather justice and love in all intimate connections. A justice-centered contemporary Christian ethic seeks, therefore, to *raise, not lower,* moral standards. Living ethically means acting in ways that strengthen our at-homeness in our bodies, enhance self-respect, deepen communication with others, and encourage whatever allows community to flourish. Toward this end, what Christians should teach is to demand *more, not less,* in terms of what is deserved and what is owed in intimate and all other connec-tions. And because a justice-love ethic encourages people not to settle for less, people become noticeably discontented with the way things are. No wonder the religious Right is so deeply agitated by the call to sexual sanity and justice making!

The concluding chapter offers further reflections on justice and love as the LBGT community and its allies try to figure out what should be done if marriage rights are won or if they are denied.

CHAPTER SEVEN

Queer Notions

> Religions are in the business of
> recommending counter-cultural
> visions of the good life.[1]
>
> — SALLIE MCFAGUE

T HIS CHAPTER STRETCHES the debate beyond equal access to marriage and calls for decentering marriage from its culturally hegemonic position. What would it mean to abolish marriage as a legal institution and focus, instead, on religious marriage? That would make sense, from a progressive Christian perspective, especially if people married not only for love, but also for justice. Marriage then would be a training school for counter-cultural resistance to unjust power and authority. At the same time, we must ask what justice requires of the LBGT community and its allies if marriage rights are denied or if they are won. Finally, what does the dual commandment to love God and neighbor as self mean in light of affirming God as the divine but definitely *unmarried* Lover?

No simple question

To evoke a clear-cut response, the entire debate about same-sex marriage is sometimes reduced to a single question: should lesbian and gay couples (be allowed to) marry, yes or no? In the process of examining the conflicting ways in which the various parties to this debate define the issues and frame their arguments, I have found that this is not an easy question to answer, at least not with a simple "yes" or "no." I have also come to believe that this may not even be the most important or interesting question to pose!

In studying this debate, I have become clearer about some things, more conflicted about others. As a gay man, I support extending the legal right to marry to same-sex couples. I also approve of making domestic partnerships and other contractual arrangements equally available to gay and non-gay couples. For most LBGT people I have talked with, this makes sense as a matter of simple justice. Same-sex couples should have access to the same status and benefits of civil marriage that heterosexual couples enjoy; they should also assume comparable responsibilities. Furthermore, as an ordained Christian minister, I have long witnessed the integrity and commitment with which lesbians and gay men enter into lifelong partnerships with the ones they love as their closest "kith and kin." For this reason, I have officiated for some years at union services for same-sex couples, and I expect to continue doing so.

My ambivalence surfaces elsewhere in terms of the justice implications of the institution of marriage. As someone who was once married heterosexually, I confess that I never found marriage personally liberating or particularly user-friendly. Perhaps that has to do with my own limitations, but I wager it has as much, if not more, to do with the problematic history of the institution and its current practice. Although formal equality in contemporary marriage is widely celebrated, in actuality marriage remains a gendered and role-differentiated arrangement. Women carry a disproportionate share of responsibilities for maintaining the household and rearing children even when they are employed outside the home.[2] Moreover, largely because of the organization of the capitalist workplace that consistently subordinates human need to profit maximization, men and increasing numbers of women who are wageworkers encounter serious structural impediments to their being actively involved in parenting or caring for aging parents.

As an advocate of justice for women, I share the feminist critique that the institution of marriage reinforces female subordination and naturalizes male gender privilege. In addition, marriage serves as the linchpin of LBGT oppression through the institutionalizing of compulsory heterosexuality, the cultural reinforcement of hierarchical gender conformity, and state regulation of sex. Although many marriages are true partnerships, by and large the institution is more associated with inequality and oppression than with justice and liberation.

For this reason, my partner and I anticipate that, if and when the marriage option becomes legally available, we will choose not to wed. But then again, who among us, myself included, can ever accurately predict where he or she will land on this issue when the legal option actually becomes available? That possibility may be sooner rather than later, given the June 2003 judicial decision in Ontario permitting marriage licenses for same-sex couples, the authorization in Belgium for lesbian and gay couples to wed, and judicial decisions pending, as of September 2003, in Massachusetts and New Jersey.

While these developments continue to unfold, it would be wise not to buy into an ahistorical essentialism that regards marriage as "only this" or "only that." Rather, the moral course of action is to get behind efforts to reform this institution in more humanizing directions, for everyone's benefit. Even so, LBGT people might be advised to withhold their support of marriage as a publicly and religiously sanctioned arrangement until they are persuaded that access to this institution can accomplish at a minimum four things: strengthen ties of mutual affection, increase positive regard for LBGT people (whether partnered or not), provide LBGT families support and stability in the midst of hard times, and energize the LBGT community to continue contributing to the betterment of society.

Marriage reservations

In *Marriage after Modernity: Christian Marriage in Postmodern Times*, Adrian Thatcher identifies two reasons for his rethinking marriage: his interest in offering "an unreserved commendation of Christian marriage," and his desire to "contribute to a renewed vision for Christian marriage at a time of unprecedented social change."[3] I share his interest in developing a renewed vision of marriage and family. Where I part company is with Thatcher's "unreserved commendation" of marriage itself.

My passionate interest in promoting gender and sexual justice prompts ambivalence about marriage as a civil and religious institution. My reluctance to commend marriage is not because people cannot or do not find joy and solace within this relational framework. As a lived covenantal relationship, marriage is strongly positive in many people's lives. I recognize and rejoice in that fact. My reservation has more to do with a historical awareness of marriage as a site of oppression and tremendous pain and suffering, both for those who engage in it and for those excluded from it. As discussed throughout this book, law, religious edict, and social custom have denied entire groups of people the freedom to marry and consequent recognition and protection for their families. Not to participate — or not to be allowed to participate — in the marital family has meant one is a loner, outsider, moral failure, social deviant, or at the very least odd.

I am particularly cautious when it is Protestant Christians who wax enthusiastic about marriage, given their tendency to sacralize "holy matrimony" as the central, person-defining rite of a comfortable bourgeois piety. I am wary because many Christians seem more invested in preserving the "sanctity of marriage" as a status of respectability than in protecting the dignity and well-being of adults and children within diverse family patterns. Moreover, I am highly doubtful that any program or set of programs aimed at enriching or "saving" marriage will ever be as effective in promoting people's well-being as would collective efforts to establish a more economically just, compassionate, and environmentally sane society.

Decentering marriage

Because of these ongoing concerns, I find myself in sync with Judith Plaskow, author of an intriguing essay entitled "Decentering Sex: Rethinking Jewish Sexual Ethics." As a lesbian feminist, Plaskow understands how difficult it is to give sex its due without reinforcing the tendency to make sex the most important aspect of human existence. She frames the challenge this way: "How can one formulate a sexual ethic that decenters sex?"[4] Similarly, I ask how we might renew a Christian ethic of intimacy and family without reinforcing compulsory coupling or giving marriage determinative weight, including its powerful role in determining benefits and protections from the state. Even though the previously discussed cultural shift toward "intimate democracy" and more egalitarian marriage and family patterns is a positive movement, too much significance is still heaped upon both sex and marriage. This is especially true within religious circles that tend to regard the marital family as the best bellwether, and full explanation, for social stresses and strains. This privatizing trend means that many religious communities have focused their attention on "personal" matters, such as spiritual growth and small group experiences. Social justice concerns are ignored or downplayed, including the morally unacceptable levels of economic disparity between rich and poor in the United States and globally. The Right has used sexuality (and race) as wedge issues to stir up conflict and encourage this abandonment of justice concerns as too conflictual and not spiritual enough.[5]

Responsible moral discourse about intimacy and family life must connect the personal and the political, refuse to privatize marriage and family (as somehow existing independently of or in isolation from other social institutions), and regard marriage reform as but one component of a larger, more comprehensive change agenda. On this score, the feminist insight that the "personal is also political" remains pivotal, suggesting that the marriage crisis should not be viewed narrowly as a matter of personal moral failure or of "dysfunctional" families, but rather as bound up with gender, race, sexual, and economic injustice throughout society. Without a critical structural analysis, it will be impossible to grasp how the quality of personal and family life is always conditioned by the wider social order. Life is shared, and our personal well-being is utterly tied up with and dependent on the well-being of others and the conditions of our communities. To keep this social justice point of view at the forefront, Christians (and others) must cease commending marriage per se and start commending, to adults of all sexualities, only ethical, justice-centered intimate partnerships based on equality and equitably shared power.

Contested claims about an evolving institution

When I first began examining the theological and public policy literature on same-sex marriage, I found it useful to jot down my own assumptions about marriage, sexuality, and religion. Although this debate seems to be about one simple question ("same-sex marriage, yes or no"), in actuality it is about much more, including contested issues about citizenship, family, democratic values, cultural mores and sexual ethics, economic and human rights, gender and sexual justice, and the connections between sexuality, spirituality, and personal/communal renewal. Although various parties to this debate would likely challenge some or all of my assumptions, I share this list to encourage readers to draw up their own. No doubt the attentive reader will notice how these assumptions have informed my entire analysis:

1. From a progressive Christian perspective, justice making lies at the heart of the moral life.

2. Historically, marriage has exhibited little by way of justice, especially for women.

3. Granting lesbians and gay men equal access to a troubled institution is not the substance of justice.

4. Justice necessitates transforming marriage in the direction of gender and sexual equality, a renewal process to which LBGT people are already contributing.

5. In sorting out the demands of gender and sexual justice, the Christian tradition may be helpful, but not without undergoing its own transformation.

6. A progressive Christian ethical framework is needed that will decenter marriage, not privilege heterosexuality, and help democratize sexuality by showing respect for a diversity of human sexualities while honoring the rich variety of ways in which people establish and sustain family.

7. Justice will be more closely approximated when marriage becomes publicly recognizable — even celebrated — as a *queer* institution

not only because it welcomes gay and non-gay couples alike, but also because it encourages people to subvert hierarchical, nonshared, and nonreciprocal power wherever it exists.

These assumptions have kept me alert to the fact that changes in marriage should be expected. We should welcome — and help bring about — changes that are in keeping with our most cherished Christian values, including the commitment to respect the dignity and worth of all persons and to resist oppression. The same-sex marriage debate offers, therefore, an opportunity to improve the climate of receptivity for equality and respect for LBGT persons, just as past marriage reforms have pressed for gender and racial equality.

Today, civil marriage is increasingly recognized as a gender-neutral partnership between two equal persons. Each individual has the status of full personhood with the right to consent to marry, to refuse to marry, and to withdraw from a marriage once contracted. Both parties have the same rights and responsibilities, to each other and to society. What continues to keep the institution of marriage relevant is, therefore, not rigid preservation of legal tradition or strict adherence to beliefs and practices from previous eras, but rather the adaptability of this institution to contemporary concerns and values.

While marriage is not infinitely elastic, it is amenable to change and should be remolded to "fit the times." This holds for religious as well as civil marriage. Jesus insisted that even the most valued institution of his Jewish tradition, the Sabbath, should be judged by whether it genuinely met human needs. Theologian Sallie McFague, echoing this admonition, suggests that "Christianity has always been most effective when it has reconstructed its doctrines in light of reality as currently understood."[6] A living tradition is one that keeps serving life as life changes.

The appropriate question to ask is not whether marriage will survive the legalizing of same-sex partnerships or the blessing of these unions religiously. Marriage no doubt will survive these and other changes. The better, more telling question is: which sorts of marriage (and family) should be encouraged, supported, and blessed? My own interest is in marriage based on mutuality and shared power, not on sex or gender inequalities. This equality model fits both same-sex and different-sex couples.

The two major objections to same-sex marriage simply no longer hold power: that marriage requires a gender hierarchy between two parties with different and unequal roles and status, and that same-sex love (and sex) is wrong, sinful, and criminal. Assumptions different from these inform the contemporary marriage reform movement. By acknowledging the full humanity of women and of LBGT as well as heterosexual persons, we can focus on a different matter altogether: not how to preserve the exclusive and excluding nature of (heterosexual, procreative) marriage, but rather how church and society might better support adult intimate partnerships and promote stable families in a world in which the composition of families is dramatically changing.

A call for a broader debate

The debate about marriage and family is much broader than the question of whether same-sex couples should be included among those eligible to marry. A lively debate is needed about a host of other issues, including the following:

- *Marriage as vocation.* How might it be possible to break with compulsory monogamy and make marriage genuinely elective, as a vocation (or calling) for some but not all? Legal scholar Nancy Polikoff tells a poignant story of a female law student who had long insisted she would not marry her heterosexual partner as long as lesbians and gay men are denied the right to marry. However, this young woman buckled under pressure when she realized she was ready to have children. Although marriage is typically presented as a "free choice" that exists alongside other, equally valid options, such as domestic partnerships and civil unions, the truth of the matter is that "long-term, voluntary, non-marital cohabitation, especially if it includes children, is not truly a choice." As Polikoff writes, "I do not blame her [for proceeding to marry]. The constraints of ideology, history and tradition . . . are powerful forces."[7]

- *Multiple partners.* Should marriage, as the legal sanctioning of an intimate sexual affiliation, be limited to two and only two persons, or should room be made for multiple partners who wish to have their intimate relationship recognized and protected by the state? Should religious communities bless multiple coexisting sexual partnerships? Surely one concern with polyamorous affiliations is exploitation, or what feminist critics of polygamy have called an "excess of patriarchy." But how exactly does the number of partners affect the moral quality of a relationship? This question requires a serious answer. Could it be that limiting intimate partnerships to only two people at a time is no guarantee of avoiding exploitation, and expanding them to include more than two parties is no guarantee that the relationship will be exploitative?

- *Ethical marriage.* The latter question leads to an even more basic question: what makes marriage (and other kinds of adult intimate relationships) ethical and just? Given the absence of a religious tradition of ethical marriage, as discussed in chapter 6, what resources might be drawn upon to answer this question? Who should have the definitional authority to determine an authentic marriage or "real" family?

- *Married bisexuals.* When bisexual persons marry heterosexually, often they are (wrongly) perceived as no longer "truly" bisexual. Similarly, when marriage becomes available to same-sex couples, will bisexual persons still be perceived as bisexual when they marry a person of their own sex?[8] This question presses the issue of why the sex or sexual orientation of intimate partners matters in the first place, to whom, and for what reasons.

- *Transsexual marriage.*[9] The reigning bipolar sex/gender paradigm reduces complex human sexualities to a fixed either/or, male/female dichotomy and fails to make room for intersexuality, transgenderism, transsexuality, and other sexualities. Is it adequate to retain a conventional definition of marriage as the union of "one man and one woman" when both law and some religions are struggling with definitions of who is male, who is female, and what delineates the human person? Recognizing that there are more than two sex/genders and a multiplicity of sexualities, Christine Gudorf asks: "In marriage legislation, should a religion recognize or perform a marriage for a woman and her transsexual fiancé (who is chromosomally female) or for a man and his chromosomally male fiancée who suffered a circumcision accident at birth and was surgically reassigned and raised as a girl from six months?"[10] These kinds of question are surfacing more and more in a pluralistic church and society.

- *Change strategies.* With regard to altering marriage and family policy, should the focus be directly on marriage itself, or should the focus be on improving the social and economic conditions that, in turn, will help strengthen family life? In speaking of the African American community, William Julius Wilson argues that it is a waste of time to focus on anything but altering the social environment in which people live their marriages and other relationships. Programs aimed at marriage promotion or developing the relational skills of couples have limited efficacy. What would go a much longer way toward strengthening families are good paying jobs with adequate benefits, decent health care, and affordable housing. Doing something worthwhile about marriage means "the society has to commit itself to a comprehensive program to address the problem of inequality. These cannot be programs that don't have a long-term basis."[11] This insight fits well with the first mentioned above, that the quality of marriage rises or falls in relation to existing social, economic, and cultural conditions and their relative fairness.

But should marriage be abolished?

Regarding intimacy, family life, and sexual justice, LBGT people have considerable wisdom to offer, including the following insights:

First, contrary to claims by some marriage advocates that winning marriage is the capstone to all efforts aimed at achieving LBGT equality, marriage itself is not the prize. The goal is justice and ending oppression of every kind.

Second, the marriage crisis is located not in the *de*valuation of marriage, as marriage traditionalists claim, but rather in its *over*valuation. Marriage has been privileged, legally and religiously speaking, to the denigration of other kinds of adult relationships, including nonsexual friendships, domestic partnerships, long-term cohabitation, and single-parent families. As a consequence of the hegemony of marriage, significant social and economic benefits are securely tied to marital status. Access to comparable benefits for the unmarried has been either limited or denied altogether.

Third, one way to ease the marriage debate "logjam" would be for heterosexual couples to begin living and acting more like their LBGT counterparts, a pattern described in chapter 5 as reverse assimilation. Why should *heterosexual* couples not be satisfied with having only the more limited legal options of domestic partnerships and civil unions? Is it not enough for different-sex couples to receive a blessing of their relationships from their religious tradition? How does a state license authorize or legitimate one's partnership? Is civil marriage really necessary (or desirable) for anyone? The same kind of questions should be asked about religious endorsement.

Abolishing marriage as a legal institution is a provocative, but not entirely far-fetched notion. The state's compelling interest in marriage and family policy has been to promote stable families and guard the safety and well-being of children, but why should the state be invested in promoting (heterosexual) marriage? The *marital family* is only one way to construct family, as current demographic studies indicate. Rather than granting the marital family special status and a monopoly of economic and social benefits, the state could emphasize not family *form* but family *function*. Surely, not one but a variety of family models deserves the community's support. As discussed in previous chapters, social scientific research amply documents that different family forms facilitate the basic family functions quite well, including successful child rearing by lesbian and gay parents. Respect for diverse families would also help decenter the conventional patriarchal family, a move in keeping with the contemporary emphasis on egalitarian marriage.

Examining alternatives to the traditional marital family, legal scholar Martha Fineman proposes replacing the marital family, which has at its core sexual (and reproductive) affiliation, with what she calls the caretaking family, which has at its core relationships of dependency and care, such as parents' care of children and adults caring for ill or aging family members.[12] The state should no longer seek to regulate (adult, consensual) sexual relationships. Rather, its constructive role is to guarantee the social and economic conditions needed so that all families will have adequate resources and the tools necessary to raise children and do the other functions that society depends upon for the well-being of its members and its own future.

Abolishing marriage as a state-subsidized institution does not mean abolishing either marriage or family. Family is not synonymous with marriage. Nonmarried persons who bond together are quite successful at fulfilling family functions, as LBGT families demonstrate. Fineman writes, "We do not need legal marriage to accomplish many societal objectives," such as nurturing children, caring for dependent adults, and sustaining domestic partners economically. By no longer privileging the marital family above other families, it would be possible to "transfer the social and economic subsidies and privilege that marriage now receives" and distribute these communal resources more equitably to what she identifies as "a new family core connection — that of the caretaker-dependent."[13]

Even if marriage were no longer a legal status, it would continue to be an important cultural institution for many people, including many religious people, because of its symbolic and expressive power. At the same time, civil marriage would no longer serve as the exclusive conduit for distributing state-conferred benefits and protections. Instead, distribution would be made on the basis of the needs and interests of caretaker-dependent family units, some of which would certainly be marital families, but not all. All families would be treated equally, and justice would be enhanced across social and cultural differences.

Marriage traditionalists are likely to regard the proposal to abolish state-sanctioned marriage as a worst-case scenario, only proving that their fears are warranted that same-sex couples wish to destroy the very institution they seek to enter. Similarly, advocates for same-sex marriage might object that efforts to dismantle civil marriage on the eve of LBGT people winning the right to marry smacks of an ill-advised, perhaps even heterosexist ploy to deprive historical outsiders of the social recognition and benefits they have been unjustly denied for so long. For their part, queer theorists and other LBGT marriage critics might applaud this move to deregulate marriage, but not all would agree that the state should keep an activist role in regulating some sexually charged activity (e.g., sexual harassment) or in guaranteeing economic benefits and legal protections for caretaker-dependent relationships.

At the same time, if marriage rights as currently defined are extended to same-sex couples, this change may end up reinforcing, not challenging, the cultural hegemony of this institution. When lesbian and gay couples are able to marry, it is likely, and some argue inevitable, that so-called "marriage light" options, such as domestic partnerships and civil unions, will drop by the wayside as second-class, less desirable choices. If so, the pressure will mount for all couples to marry, only reinforcing marriage's institutional status as the exclusive conduit for state subsidies and social respectability. Lesbians and gay men who choose not to marry will be further stigmatized, along with their nonmarrying heterosexual counterparts.

In my judgment, a thoroughly revised legal and ethical framework is needed that does not rely exclusively on marriage as the signifier of family, but recognizes intentionally diverse networks of people committed to each other's well-being.[14] Families are formed not because the state issues a license or a religious ceremony is conducted, but because people exercise their moral agency to bond for loving, mutual care. If marriage were ended as a state-defined and regulated institution, would it not be reasonable to expect that the state would strongly decrease, if not stop altogether, its efforts to regulate sexual affiliations between consenting adults?[15] The law would retain its

interest in protecting vulnerable persons from sexual harm and violation, but the state's concern would be to curtail sexual exploitation
and abuse, not curtail sexuality, especially that of minoritized groups.
The proper focus of public policy would be on guaranteeing the political and economic conditions so that all people might participate in
and contribute to community life. Contrary to the dismissive claims
of marriage traditionalists, society has great need for its LBGT members. So does the church. This shift might have additional benefits, as
well. It might help religious traditions get clear that the moral problem is not (and never has been) sex, but rather sexual alienation,
exploitation, and abuse.

Should marriage be religious only?

In speaking about state authorization of marriage thirty years after the
historic U.S. Supreme Court decision in *Loving v. Virginia,* which declared that laws banning interracial marriage were unconstitutional,
legal scholar Stephen Carter has argued that marriage should be regarded primarily as a religious institution. Furthermore, the denial by
the state of a couple's right to marriage should be seen as a violation
of their religious freedom. Although various U.S. states prior to 1967
had banned "mixed race" marriages, Carter insists that if an interracial
couple was "married in a church, was married in the eyes of God, the
fact that the state refused to recognize their union or even sought to
punish it, did not make it any less a marriage." The marriage would be
recognized as valid because a duly authorizing religious body conferred
it. Not to do so makes "the state oppressive and even idiotic."[16]

The essential question is, "Why is the state in the business of
regulating marriage at all?"[17] Carter bemoans the fact that religious
organizations have, in his words, "surrendered" fundamental authority
over "the most basic form of human relationship." He attributes the
weakening of marriage as an institution to its entrapment as "part of
our political and regulatory culture," which means "it has lost the hard
solemn edge that it traditionally had and should continue to have."[18]
In proposing to repeal civil marriage law, he acknowledges that this

is "an idea, I think it's fair to say, that nobody likes," but he puts it forward. He also argues that it is necessary to retain only law that covers the dissolution of marriages. "The One Big Marriage Law," as he calls it, would provide "that whatever private institution marries you also gets to decide what happens if you decide to seek a divorce. Thus the One Big Marriage Law provides an incentive to think really hard about where and how to get married."[19]

If marriage were no longer defined and regulated by the state, then religious groups, among others, would need to articulate how their theologies of marriage provide, functionally, more than a mere solemnizing of what the state establishes by issuing a formal license. The pivotal questions would become these: What business, if any, does religion have in "performing" marriage? If it has legitimate business, which kinds of relationship should be recognized as valid unions and, therefore, be blessed?[20]

As a progressive Protestant Christian, I would encourage my tradition and others to think of marriage in two primary ways. First, celebrating a marriage publicly in a religious ceremony should affirm the partners' intention to make a life together as lovers and co-equal contributors to a more just world, including a more just church. Second, and in keeping with this emphasis, marriage should signify the couple's (and their sponsoring community's) pledge "from this day forward, for better for worse, for richer for poorer, in sickness and in health" to resist oppressive authorities and struggle together to maximize justice and dignity for all persons and the earth's care. Loving well also requires an ongoing commitment to seek justice in all things, which means there will always be a public as well as a more personal, even private, face to any marital covenanting. Religious traditions should encourage and equip people to marry not for love, but for love *and* justice.

From a progressive Christian perspective, ethically sound marriage is about counter-cultural resistance, not a quest for legitimation of one's life (or love) by the state. At the same time, a religious ceremony is called for, because the gathered faith community offers a blessing in order to express gratitude to God for these people and in recognition of the joy and courage of their union. Juan Oliver, in speaking of the liturgical challenge to subvert church rituals that demean LBGT persons, wonders how churches might encourage "the reintegration of outcasts" and the reformation of more inclusive, welcoming communities. The main question to sort out, he suggests, is "How and why is the Christian assembly grateful to God for creating Gay and Lesbian people and manifesting God's love in ours?"[21]

Celebrating LBGT love as resistance to moral evil

Celebrating the lives and love of LBGT people is without doubt a departure from much conventional religious practice. In another sense, it is something remarkably traditional, given the longstanding theological conviction that where love is found, there is God.[22] Similarly, where there is un-love, injustice, and oppression, there people are called to resistance. Resistance includes entering into and sustaining solidarity with those harmed by status quo arrangements and demeaned by conventional wisdom. It also requires naming as moral evil whatever violates persons' bodies and spirits and breaks the relational web of life that connects one to another and to the earth.

Theologian James Poling points out that "evil is systemic and organized at every level of human life, including the religious level."[23] In fact, evil often uses religion as a mask to hide and make it appear as if evil is not really evil but rather something virtuous and just, even loving. Insisting, as many religious people do, that marriage is an exclusively heterosexual institution is an example of how evil masks itself as reasonable and virtuous. Without access to a counter-story and counter-theology to name heterosexism as morally evil, religious communities fail to recognize evil as truly evil. When evil is not seen and named, it cannot be resisted.

In a religiously shaped marriage culture that has naturalized the "union of one man and one woman" as alone godly, what would it require to resist evil and, even more, to begin to "organize goodness"? At least three things come to mind.

First, a justice spirituality calls for "intentional disestablishment," theologian Douglas John Hall's phrase for standing on the margins to protest injustice and demand redress.[24] For many conventionally religious groups, marginality signals only loss and diminishment, but it can also be a site of freedom for new vision (to see things differently) and to practice freedom (to try out new experiments in intimate and communal living).

Second, no ethic or theology should dare focus exclusively on a single moral evil or injustice. Evil exists as a web of interstructured injustices, each complicating and reinforcing the others. While strategically it may be wise to focus on what causes immediate endangerment to one's own group or community, a more comprehensive justice framework appreciates that anti-racism work requires anti-sexism work, which requires anti-heterosexism work, which requires anti-classism work, and so forth.

Third, the evil to be resisted is not only the evil done to us, but also the evil we do, often unconsciously. The salient point is that we have not lost the moral capacity to make choices, including choices about how to spend our relative social power and privilege. Nor have we lost our moral freedom to be held accountable for those choices.

What if access to marriage is denied or won?

As marriage advocates press to acquire the freedom to marry for same-sex couples, and as LBGT people insist on full recognition of their families, we must consider various scenarios for LBGT people and their heterosexual allies, depending on whether they win or fail to win marriage rights.

If current public policy is not altered, the immediate issue for heterosexual allies will be staying in solidarity with the LBGT community. Some clergy have challenged their denomination's policies and officiated at union services for lesbian and gay couples. For their courageous stance, some have been brought to ecclesiastical trial.[25] Other clergy have elected not to function as agents of the state in signing marriage licenses until full marriage rights are available to same-sex couples. Instead, they perform only the religious ceremony and leave it to others, such as a justice of the peace, to sign the marriage certificate registering the marriage civilly.[26] Congregations have developed other strategies, including revisiting their marriage and wedding policies and updating them to be LBGT-supportive. As a consequence, some have opted to no longer offer marriage ceremonies, but rather only union or covenanting services without any religious distinction made between same-sex and different-sex unions. If couples wish to marry legally and have that option, they may negotiate that transaction outside the faith community.

My hope for LBGT people confronting the denial of full marriage and family rights is that they not become preoccupied with this issue to the neglect of other justice concerns. Of special urgency these days is entitlement to basic economic and legal protections for all members of society, whether married or not. Our change agenda (and here I speak as a professional, white gay man) should not focus on acquiring (more) privilege and social status. Rather, we must build stronger multicultural coalitions to pursue a wide justice agenda that challenges white racism, cultural elitism, global economic disparities, escalating militarization, and ecological degradation. While our analysis must decipher the ideologically loaded politics of marriage, it must also provide a cogent critique of other public policy issues, such as the 1996 national welfare reform legislation that promotes marriage as a private, individualized solution for the public, communal problem of poverty.[27] On every issue, the implications of race and economic justice must be considered.

A victory of full marriage rights will produce other challenges. For heterosexual allies, the loss of exclusive marital entitlement and unearned heterosexual privilege will be a bitter pill for many of their compatriots, who may be manipulated into an organized backlash by the Right. Many, perhaps most heterosexual persons have had few incentives to imagine life without the freedom to marry. It often takes a moral shock of some sort to stretch someone's imagination. Perhaps the passage of LBGT-friendly marriage legislation, favorable judicial decisions, and more publicly celebrated religious unions of same-sex couples will provide that necessary jolt to begin perceiving how state-regulated marriage has diminished a sexual minority while elevating the majority. Because so many heterosexuals take marriage for granted, they have tended to regard their decisions to marry as private choices with personal meaning only. Our heterosexual allies will need to conduct a grassroots educational campaign to explain to other heterosexuals why nothing could be further from the truth.

As the LBGT community acquires marriage rights, the challenge will be not to trade freedom for respectability. Fifty years ago, in one of the early homophile magazines, E. B. Saunders wrote that joining the marriage bandwagon might actually be a move to limit rather than expand freedom. In his words, "Rebels such as we, demand freedom! But actually we have a greater freedom now (sub rosa as it may be) than do heterosexuals and any change will be to lose some of it in return for respectability. Are we willing to make that trade?"[28] Because marginality offers the possibility of alternative vision and freedom to experiment with new forms of relationship and family, giving up marginality exacts a price. A related challenge will be not breaking ranks with those LBGT adults who choose not to marry. Solidarity within the community will require conscientious efforts on several different fronts.

The unmarried divine Lover

For many within the LBGT community, myself included, the desire and capacity to keep on loving and struggling for justice, for ourselves and others, is sustained by the movement of the Spirit that keeps hope alive. In a definition of the Jesus movement that I find appealing, ethicist Larry Rasmussen speaks of a community called to "creative deviance on the frontline."[29] Why deviance? Because it does not accept the standard definitions. Why creative? Because it seeks out real alternatives. And frontline? Because the community stays engaged in the hard, ongoing, and messy work of seeking a different world and a different church. This community is loyal to the God who is Love, but also the divine Lover. This latter theological naming has particular significance for progressive Christians who seek to weigh in on the same-sex marriage question.

Affirming God as Lover may be jarring because of the erotic overtones of the word "lover," but this term is commonplace in Christian mystical writings. Theologian Sallie McFague in *Models of God* argues in favor of using this precise God language in spite of the fear because "God as lover is the moving power of the universe, the desire for unity with all the beloved, the passionate embrace that spins the 'living pulsing earth' around, sends the 'blood through our veins,' and 'draws us into one another's arms.' "[30] Moreover, the erotic is a dimension of divinely created love without which life itself becomes cold, heartless, and boring.

The telling question is not whether God is Lover, but rather what kind of lover is holy, powerful, and worthy of praise. The answer to that question goes a long way toward informing us of the kinds of lover that we, too, are called to be. Here, as elsewhere in the religious tradition, there are choices. "Lover" may mean the jealous, possessive spouse who punishes or threatens to punish the intimate other. Biblical scholars have detailed the destructive image of this abusive batterer-God.[31] The divine Lover may also refer to the traditional depiction of the unmarried God, neither husband nor wife to a divine consort, but the One who loves beyond, outside, and unbounded by marriage.[32] The fact also that Jesus is never recorded in any of the New Testament traditions as married and, further, is often characterized as at odds with his own biological family, only further complicates matters for a religious tradition that has come perilously close to sacralizing marriage.[33] However, the most unnerving image of all may be of the God who is both unmarried *and* promiscuous, the divine Lover whose love is not limited to only certain people or groups, but rather expansively takes in all of creation.

This image of God as unmarried, promiscuous lover, while not the only God image to retain, has relevance in our context as a reminder not to invest overly in marriage as an identity-defining category. From a progressive Christian perspective, far less attention should be given to culturally prescribed identities and far more to socially liberatory practices. What matters ethically, religiously is not who or what we are, but the quality of our actions toward self and others.

The miracle — and subversive power — of big love

During the 2000 legislative session in Vermont that led to the establishment of civil unions as a parallel institution to marriage ("everything but the name"), Representative Bill Lippert, the state's only openly gay legislator, spoke during the rancorous floor debate in order, as he said, to "put a face" on the issue. "Gay and lesbian people and gay and lesbian couples deserve not only rights, they deserve to be celebrated," he told his legislative colleagues and the onlookers in the chamber. "Our lives, in the midst of historic prejudice and historic discrimination, are to my view, in some ways, miracles." To resist the cultural hatred that bombards them daily and, at the same time, to retain the desire and capacity to love is, Lippert concluded, "a triumph" of the spirit and goodness of LBGT people.[34]

All talk of love, whether about partnership, marriage, or family, should also be justice talk. It should take into account how the lack of personal well-being and dignity, so much in evidence in this culture, is utterly conditioned by social and economic injustice. Oppression inflicts suffering. It also constricts people's natural affections to a narrow, often closed circle of intimates and friends. In a culture split apart by white racial supremacy, male gender supremacy, homophobia, and economic greed, it sadly makes sense that people rarely exhibit what Patricia Hill Collins calls "big love."[35] Big loving depends on wildly expansive justice making and putting the social, economic, and cultural conditions in place that foster respect and trust among people. Justice-love is more securely in place when men truly value women as themselves, when whites cherish the humanity of people of color, and when men-loving-men and women-loving-women are treasured as honored family and community members.

When oppression is not resisted, human love becomes smaller and narrowly circumscribed. People become preoccupied with safety and control. Because our deepest yearnings for love can be satisfied only when our moral commitments are also enlarged, we must demand re-spect for ourselves and engage in justice struggles, for our sake and the sake of others, with our whole bodies, minds, and spirits. In doing so, we discover, happily, that justice making makes love more pleasurable.

To be candid, few queer people are yet persuaded that marriage can be a school for love or justice. The final verdict is not in. In the meantime, because of our disloyalty to the regime of compulsory heterosexual monogamy, we are feared and punished. We are also feared because our animating passion is to break the hold of each and every oppression. The so-called gay agenda, so trivialized and distorted by the religious Right, is far less about marriage and far more about seeking an expansive justice that includes all. Toward this end, our life-vocation is to recruit as many people as possible, regardless of age, color, class, sexuality, or marital status, to join our brilliantly multicultural, multicolored justice movement.

Guardians of the sexual status quo fear that this queer passion for justice-love may catch on and "corrupt" others, especially youth. After all, self-respecting and erotically empowered people are often willing to take risks for love and to make a difference. They tend also to refuse to settle for less than what they and all other people deserve: a fabu-lously inclusive world (and church) that welcomes friends, lovers, and strangers and seeks to turn this precious globe into a nurturing home for all. Be forewarned, therefore: when people come to love justice this deeply, this passionately, they become justifiably and dangerously queer, no matter whether they are LBGT or not and, most definitely, whether they are married or not.

Notes

Introduction

1. Adrienne Rich, *Arts of the Possible: Essays and Conversations* (New York: W. W. Norton, 2001), 164.

2. Throughout this book I use a variety of terms that are less than satisfactory. Although I speak of "same-sex marriage," that phrase does not indicate a separate category of marriage (so-called gay marriage as distinct from "straight" or heterosexual marriage) but rather refers to a marriage involving two men or two women. I presume these couples are homoerotically attracted and sexually active. Furthermore, when I use the collective term "gay people," I am referring not only to homosexual men, but also to lesbian women and sometimes also to bisexuals and transgender people. I also employ the acronym LBGT (lesbian, bisexual, gay, and transgender) even though how those letters are sequenced is debated. Making justice is complicated, among other reasons, because we have no innocent or pure language unaffected by the injustices of the prevailing sex/gender system.

3. Both the Robertson spokesperson and Sheldon are quoted by Evan Wolfson, "How to Win the Freedom to Marry," *Harvard Gay and Lesbian Review* 4, no. 4 (Fall 1997): 30.

4. Gabriel Rotello, "To Have and to Hold: The Case for Gay Marriage," *Nation*, June 24, 1996, 16.

5. E. J. Graff, "Retying the Knot," *Nation*, June 24, 1996, 12.

6. For exceptions, see Margaret A. Farley, *Personal Commitments: Beginning, Keeping, Changing* (San Francisco: Harper & Row, 1990); Eugene F. Rogers, Jr., *Sexuality and the Christian Body: Their Way into the Triune God* (Malden, Mass.: Blackwell Publishers, 1999); and Elizabeth Stuart, *Just Good Friends: Towards a Lesbian and Gay Theology of Relationships* (London: Mowbray, 1995). See also Christian Batalden Scharen, *Married in the Sight of God: Theology, Ethics, and Church Debates over Homosexuality* (Lanham, Md.: University Press of America, 2000); and Anne Bathurst Gilson, *The Battle for America's Families: A Feminist Response to the Religious Right* (Cleveland: Pilgrim Press, 1999).

7. Marvin M. Ellison, *Erotic Justice: A Liberating Ethic of Sexuality* (Louisville: Westminster John Knox Press, 1996).

8. Rita Brock, "Marriage Troubles," in *Body and Soul: Rethinking Sexuality as Justice-Love*, ed. Marvin M. Ellison and Sylvia Thorson-Smith (Cleveland: Pilgrim Press, 2003), 352–53.

9. For a discussion of DOMA, see Carlos A. Ball, *The Morality of Gay Rights: An Exploration in Political Philosophy* (New York: Routledge, 2003); William N. Eskridge, Jr., *Equality Practice: Civil Unions and the Future of Gay Rights* (New York: Routledge, 2002); and Yuval Merin, *Equality for Same-Sex Couples: The Legal Recognition of Gay Partnerships in Europe and the United States* (Chicago: University of Chicago Press, 2002).

10. National Gay and Lesbian Task Force, "Specific Anti-Same-Sex Marriage Laws in the U.S. — June 2001," www.ngltf.org. The state of Texas passed its restrictive legislation in 1973.

11. Chris Glaser, "Marriage as We See It," *Newsweek*, September 16, 1996, 19. My emphasis.

12. Ball, *The Morality of Gay Rights*, ix.

13. The phrase "definitional authority" is taken from Cheshire Calhoun, *Feminism, the Family, and the Politics of the Closet: Lesbian and Gay Displacement* (Oxford: Oxford University Press, 2000), 131.

14. Tracey Tyler and Tracy Huffman, "Gay Couple Married after Ruling," *Toronto Star*, June 11, 2003, A4; Estanislao Oziewicz, "Same-Sex Married Couples Rejoice," *Globe and Mail*, June 11, 2003; and Clifford Krauss, "Gay Canadians' Quest for Marriage Seems Near Victory," *New York Times*, June 15, 2003, A3.

15. Supreme Court of the United States, *John Geddes Lawrence and Tyron Garner, Petitioners v. Texas*, no. 02-102, June 26, 2003, 18.

16. Ibid., Justice Scalia dissenting.

Chapter One / Marriage Changes

1. Laura L. Carstensen and Marilyn Yalom, "Introduction," in *Inside the American Couple: New Thinking, New Challenges*, ed. Marilyn Yalom and Laura L. Carstensen (Berkeley: University of California Press, 2002), 10.

2. For critical historical analyses of marriage and family, the vast literature includes Stephanie Coontz, *The Social Origins of Private Life: A History of American Families 1600–1900* (London: Verso, 1988), and *The Way We Really Are: Coming to Terms with America's Changing Families* (New York: Basic Books, 1997); Nancy Cott, *Public Vows: A History of Marriage and the Nation* (Cambridge: Harvard University Press, 2000); John D'Emilio and Estelle B. Freedman, *Intimate Matters: A History of Sexuality in America* (New York: Harper & Row, 1988); Mary Ann Glendon, *The Transformation of Family Law: State, Law, and Family in the United States and Western Europe* (Chicago: University of Chicago Press, 1989); Lawrence Stone, *The Family, Sex, and Marriage in England 1500–1800* (New York: Harper & Row, 1977); and John Witte, Jr., *From Sacrament to Contract: Marriage, Religion, and Law in the Western Tradition* (Louisville: Westminster John Knox Press, 1997).

3. The first senator cited is Phil Gramm of Texas, a Republican; the second is Robert Byrd of West Virginia, a Democrat. Excerpts from the Senate debate on the Defense of Marriage Act are found in *Same-Sex Marriage: Pro and Con*, ed. Andrew Sullivan (New York: Vintage Books, 1997), 229–38.

4. Gloria H. Albrecht, *Hitting Home: Feminist Ethics, Women's Work, and the Betrayal of "Family Values"* (New York: Continuum, 2002).

5. Michael S. Wald, "Same-Sex Couples: Marriage, Families, and Children: An Analysis of Proposition 22, The 'Knight' Initiative" (December 1999). Online see www.buddybuddy.com/wald-1.html.

6. GLAD, "Civil Marriage for Same-Sex Couples: The Facts" (Boston: Gay and Lesbian Advocates and Defenders, August 2002), 12. Online see www.glad.org/Publications/CivilRightProject/CivilMarriage_TheFacts.PDF.

7. E. J. Graff, *What Is Marriage For? The Strange Social History of Our Most Intimate Institution* (Boston: Beacon Press, 1999), 31 and 32.

8. GLAD, "Equal Marriage from Five Angles" (Boston: Gay and Lesbian Advocates and Defenders), www.glad.org/Publications/publications_lgbt.shtml.

9. GLAD, "Civil Marriage for Same-Sex Couples," 3.

10. Ibid., 2.

11. National Center for Health Statistics, "Advance Report for Final Divorce Statistics, 1989 and 1990," *Monthly Vital Statistics Report* 43, no. 9, supplement (March 22, 1995): 4.

12. Carstensen and Yalom, "Introduction," 8.

13. Ibid.

14. Rosemary Radford Ruether, *Christianity and the Making of the Modern Family* (Boston: Beacon Press, 2000), 175 and n. 62, 276, where she cites her source for this data.

15. Ibid., 6.

16. Jason Fields and Lynne M. Casper, "America's Families and Living Arrangements: Population Characteristics," *Current Population Reports 2000* (Washington, D.C.: U.S. Census Bureau, June 2001), 1.

17. Ibid., 9. In 1970, the median age at which people first married was 20.8 years for women, 23.2 years for men; by 2000, these ages had risen to 25.1 years for women, 26.8 for men.

18. Richard Quebedeaux, "The Postmodern Family," *Book World* 12 (1990), at World & I Archives, www.worldandi.com/specialreport/1990/december/Sa17142.htm.

19. Ibid.

20. John D'Emilio and Estelle B. Freedman, *Intimate Matters: A History of Sexuality in America* (New York: Harper & Row, 1988).

21. Adrian Thatcher, *Marriage after Modernity: Christian Marriage in Postmodern Times* (Sheffield, U.K.: Sheffield Academic Press, 1999), 10.

22. Task Force on Changing Families of the Advisory Committee on Social Witness Policy, *Changing Families: A Churchwide Study Document* (Louisville: Presbyterian Church [U.S.A.], 2001), 19.

23. Fields and Casper, "America's Families and Living Arrangements," 9–10.

24. Ibid.

25. Task Force on Changing Families, *Changing Families*, 19.

26. *U.S. Census Bureau News*, April 13, 1998, 1.

27. Ibid., 20.

28. "Table 8: Marital Status and Living Arrangements," *1998 Current Population Reports*, U.S. Bureau of the Census, March 1998.

29. Wald, "Same-Sex Couple Marriages and Family Policy," n. 39.

30. In *Same-Sex Unions in Premodern Europe* (New York: Villard Books, 1994) Boswell contended that same-sex unions were widespread in the premodern world. Because heterosexual marriages were often economic and/or political transactions between dynastic families or wealthy property owners, he also suggested that "ordinary men and women were more likely to invest feelings the twentieth century would call 'romantic' in *same-sex* relationships, either passionate friendships or more structured and institutional unions" (my emphasis). Boswell was also persuaded that ceremonies in the past functioned to celebrate what we would today call gay marriages: "In

almost every age and place the ceremony fulfilled what most people today regard as the essence of marriage: a permanent romantic commitment between two people, witnessed and recognized by the community" (280 and 281).

31. Faith D'Aluisio and Peter Menzel, *Women in the Material World* (San Francisco: Sierra Club Books, 1996), 38.

32. William N. Eskridge, Jr., *Equality Practice: Civil Unions and the Future of Gay Rights* (New York: Routledge, 2002), esp. chap. 3, "Comparative Law Lessons for the Same-Sex Marriage Movement," 83–126. Dutch public policy is cited on page 97.

33. Helen Oppenheimer, "Marriage," in *The Westminster Dictionary of Christian Ethics*, ed. John F. Childress and John Macquarrie (Philadelphia: Westminster Press, 1986), 366.

34. Evan Wolfson, interviewed in *Marriage — Just a Piece of Paper?* ed. Katherine Anderson, Don Browning, and Brian Boyer (Grand Rapids, Mich.: William B. Eerdmans, 2002), 349.

35. Ibid.

36. John Witte, Jr., in *Marriage — Just a Piece of Paper?* 410.

37. Nancy F. Cott, *Public Vows: A History of Marriage and the Nation* (Cambridge, Mass.: Harvard University Press, 2000), 2.

38. Wolfson, in *Marriage — Just a Piece of Paper?* 350.

39. Cott, *Public Vows*, 3.

40. Thatcher, *Marriage after Modernity*, 9, 19.

41. Cott, *Public Vows*, 3.

42. Eskridge, *Equality Practice*, 18–25; Cott, *Public Vows*, 217.

43. Martha C. Nussbaum, *Sex and Social Justice* (New York: Oxford University Press, 1999), 202.

44. Ibid., 41.

45. Beverly Harrison and James Harrison, "Some Problems for Normative Christian Family Ethics," *American Society of Christian Ethics: 1977 Selected Papers*, 77.

46. Ibid., 74.

47. Richard D. Mohr, *A More Perfect Union: Why Straight America Must Stand Up for Gay Rights* (Boston: Beacon Press, 1994), 41.

48. Ibid., 43–44.

49. Ibid., 46.

50. Lynne M. Casper and Suzanne M. Bianchi, *Continuity and Change in the American Family* (Thousand Oaks, Calif.: Sage Publications, 2002), xiii–xiv.

51. Ibid., xv–xvi.

52. James Davison Hunter, *Culture Wars: The Struggle to Define America* (New York: Basic Books, 1991).

53. Casper and Bianchi, *Continuity and Change*, xvi.

54. Cott, *Public Vows*, 202.

55. Ibid., 212.

Chapter Two / A Justice Lens

1. Karen Lebacqz, *Justice in an Unjust World: Foundations for a Christian Approach to Justice* (Minneapolis: Augsburg, 1987), 11.

2. Sallie McFague in *Life Abundant: Rethinking Theology and Economy for a Planet in Peril* (Minneapolis: Fortress Press, 2001) argues that theology's purpose is to "help us imagine and live a different abundant life," one in which just and sustainable planetary living is possible. However, North American middle-class Christians, the audience she addresses in her book, will not "live differently" unless they are able to "think differently," outside the box of capitalist and consumerist market ideology that "has become our way of life, almost our religion" (xiv, xi).

3. Pamela K. Brubaker in *Globalization at What Price? Economic Change and Daily Life* (Cleveland: Pilgrim Press, 2001) points out that of the world's top one hundred economies, fifty-one are corporations, forty-nine nation-states.

4. See Don S. Browning, *Marriage and Modernization: How Globalization Threatens Marriage and What to Do about It* (Grand Rapids, Mich.: William B. Eerdmans, 2003), esp. chap. 9, "World Family Strategies," 211–44. Although I do not share all of Browning's analysis, I do share his appreciation for the innovative advocacy and educational work of the Religious Consultation on Population, Reproductive Health, and Ethics, chaired by progressive Roman Catholic theologian Daniel C. Maguire. The Consultation's website is www.religiousconsultation.org. For a critical discussion of Browning's liberal familism, see Gloria Albrecht's *Hitting Home: Feminist Ethics, Women's Work, and the Betrayal of "Family Values"* (New York: Continuum, 2002), esp. 145–48 ("Family Values in Liberal Christianity").

5. Paz is quoted in Larry L. Rasmussen, *Moral Fragments and Moral Community: A Proposal for Church in Society* (Minneapolis: Fortress Press, 1993), 9.

6. Beverly Wildung Harrison, "Sexism and the Contemporary Church: When Evasion Becomes Complicity," in *Sexism, Religion, and Women in the Church: No More Silence!* ed. Alice L. Hageman (New York: Association Press, 1974), 195.

7. Susan Moller Okin, *Justice, Gender, and the Family* (New York: Basic Books, 1989), 135.

8. Mary McClintock Fulkerson, *Changing the Subject: Women's Discourses and Feminist Theology* (Minneapolis: Fortress Press, 1994).

9. Okin, *Justice, Gender, and the Family*, 135.

10. Ibid.

11. Suzanne Pharr, *In the Time of the Right: Reflections on Liberation* (Berkeley, Calif.: Chardon Press, 1996), 80.

12. William N. Eskridge, Jr., *Equality Practice: Civil Unions and the Future of Gay Rights* (New York: Routledge, 2002), 1. State persecution was not the only response. Social historians are documenting the not-so-hidden subculture of homoerotically attracted men in the late nineteenth and twentieth centuries in which tolerance, even covert celebration, was facilitated by the same public officials who would never have tolerated such sexual freedom for "nice white women." See George Chauncey, *Gay New York: Gender, Urban Culture, and the Making of the Gay Male World, 1890–1940* (New York: Basic Books, 1994); also Lillian Faderman, *Odd Girls and Twilight Lovers: A History of Lesbian Life in Twentieth-Century America* (New York: Columbia University Press, 1991).

13. Not every jurisdiction prosecuted sodomy laws, and heterosexual couples have rarely been subjected to state regulation. See Yuval Merin, *Equality for Same-Sex Couples: The Legal Recognition of Gay Partnerships in Europe and the United States* (Chicago: University of Chicago Press, 2002), 319.

14. As of June 2003, thirty-five states and the District of Columbia either had no sodomy law or did not enforce laws on the books because the courts had declared the laws unconstitutional. Eleven states still had laws that prohibited sodomy by same-sex couples and heterosexual couples. Four states prohibited sodomy only by same-sex couples. For details, see "The Right to Privacy," National Gay and Lesbian Task Force (www.ngltf.org/issues or write to NGLTF, 1325 Massachusetts Avenue N.W., Suite 600, Washington, DC 20005). With the U.S. Supreme Court's *Lawrence v. Texas* decision, announced late June 2003, sodomy laws across the country were declared unconstitutional.

15. David L. Chambers, "Couples: Marriage, Civil Union, and Domestic Partnership," in *Creating Change: Sexuality, Public Policy, and Civil Rights,* ed. John D'Emilio, William B. Turner, and Urvashi Vaid (New York: St. Martin's Press, 2000), 288.

16. Susan Thistlethwaite in a provocative essay entitled "Enemy Mine: Why the Religious Right Needs Homophobia" (*Chicago Theological Seminary Register: The Gilberto Castaneda Lectures 1998–2001, Countering Homophobia in Bible and Theology,* ed. Scott Haldeman, 91, no. 3 [2001]: 33–40), examines four reasons that religious conservatives hold fast to compulsory heterosexuality in its anti-gay crusade: (1) in a religious system of terror, homophobia helps to define and enforce sexual identity through establishing rigid sexual boundaries, (2) it serves as protection from a wrathful God who punishes enemies, (3) it provides the rationale for an effective means of fundraising, and (4) it functions as a mechanism that heterosexism finds useful to symbolize — and manage — forbidden sexuality.

17. Nan D. Hunter, "Sexual Dissent and the Family: The Sharon Kowalski Case (1991)," in *Sex Wars: Sexual Dissent and Political Culture,* ed. Lisa Duggan and Nan D. Hunter (London and New York: Routledge, 1995), 101–6.

18. Hunter, "Banned in the U.S.A.: What the Hardwick Ruling Will Mean (1986)," in *Sex Wars,* 81.

19. Merin, *Equality for Same-Sex Couples,* 220–22. My emphasis.

20. As of this writing (June 2003), legal cases are pending in Massachusetts and New Jersey. The Massachusetts Supreme Judicial Court has heard arguments that the right to marry the person of one's choice is a protected right under the state constitution and that the exclusion of same-sex couples from marriage and the hundreds of benefits and protections it provides is unjustified. Gay and Lesbian Advocates and Defenders (GLAD) filed the Massachusetts lawsuit in behalf of seven same-sex couples. One of the couples has been together thirty years, four couples are raising children, and another couple has grown children and now grandchildren. Ten friend of the court briefs (amici curiae) have been filed in support of the GLAD brief and represent an array of institutions and supporters: (1) the Boston Bar Association, (2) the Greater Boston Civil Rights Coalition, (3) the Urban League of Eastern Massachusetts, (4) the Massachusetts Black Women Attorneys, (5) Massachusetts NOW, (6) the Massachusetts Association of Hispanic Attorneys, (7) the American Psychoanalytic Association, (8) the National Association of Social Workers, (9) the pediatric chairs of several major hospitals, (10) authors of a leading family law treatise, (11) the Jewish Reconstructionist Federation, (12) and the Unitarian Universalist Association, as well as individual clergy from a variety of faith traditions. For additional information, see www.glad.org.

21. Laura L. Carstensen and Marilyn Yalom, "Introduction," in *Inside the American Couple: New Thinking, New Challenges*, ed. Marilyn Yalom and Laura L. Carstensen (Berkeley: University of California Press, 2002), 4.

22. Ibid., 9. My emphasis.

23. Lebacqz, *Justice in an Unjust World*: "My interest," she explains, "is not to describe and analyze the ills of the world, but to change it for the better, to create justice out of injustice. I begin with injustice not because it is 'more interesting' or offers better 'theoretical insights,' but because it is the only honest place to begun, given the realities of our world" (11). At the book's conclusion, she returns to this point: "Precisely because I take most seriously the epistemological privilege of the oppressed, I have begun with the reality of oppression and injustice as it is experienced in the world. Once one begins there, a different understanding of justice emerges" (160).

24. Marcus Borg in *Meeting Jesus Again for the First Time: The Historical Jesus and the Heart of Contemporary Faith* (San Francisco: HarperSanFrancicso, 1994), describes the difference between conventional and alternative wisdom as they inform contrasting notions of spirituality and politics and speaks of Jesus as a teacher of alternative wisdom (esp. chap. 4, 69–95).

25. In an essay entitled "Theological Reflection in the Struggle for Liberation: A Feminist Perspective" (*Making the Connections: Essays in Feminist Social Ethics*, ed. Carol S. Robb [Boston: Beacon Press, 1985]), Beverly Harrison writes of solidarity this way: "Genuine solidarity involves not mere subjective identification with oppressed people but concrete answerability to them. Solidarity *is* accountability, and accountability means being vulnerable, capable of being changed by the oppressed, welcoming their capacity to critique and alter our reality" (244).

26. Daniel C. Maguire, *The Moral Core of Judaism and Christianity: Reclaiming the Revolution* (Minneapolis: Fortress Press, 1993), 127.

27. Ibid.

28. Ibid., 63.

29. Ibid., 58.

30. Nancy Fraser, *Justice Interruptus: Critical Reflections on the "Postsocialist" Condition* (New York: Routledge, 1997), 15.

31. Cheshire Calhoun in *Feminism, the Family, and the Politics of the Closet* (New York: Oxford University Press, 2000) contends that gay oppression is best understood using the rubric of displacement: "The principal, damaging effect of a heterosexist system," she writes, "is that it *displaces* lesbians and gays from both the public and private spheres of civil society so that lesbians and gays have no legitimate social location, not even a disadvantaged one" (2).

32. Nancy Fraser, *Justice Interruptus*, 15.

33. Gary David Comstock, *Violence against Lesbians and Gay Men* (New York: Columbia University Press, 1991).

34. Iris Marion Young, *Justice and the Politics of Difference* (Princeton, N.J.: Princeton University Press, 1990), 41.

35. Ibid., 41, 42.

36. Peggy McIntosh, "White Privilege: Unpacking the Invisible Knapsack," *Peace and Freedom*, July–August 1989, 10.

37. Ibid., 12.

38. See Marvin M Ellison, *Erotic Justice: A Liberating Ethic of Sexuality* (Louisville: Westminster John Knox Press, 1996), chap. 1 ("Rethinking Sexuality: An Issue of Justice"), esp. 24–29.

39. Martha Minow, "All in the Family and in All Families: Membership, Loving, and Owing," in *Sex, Preference, and Family: Essays on Law and Nature,* ed. David M. Estlund and Martha C. Nussbaum (New York: Oxford University Press, 1997), 252.

Chapter Three / Marriage Traditionalists

1. Stanley N. Kurtz, "What Is Wrong with Gay Marriage," *Commentary,* September 2000, 7–8.

2. David W. Dunlap, "Some States Trying to Stop Gay Marriages before They Start," *New York Times,* March 15, 1995, A18.

3. William N. Eskridge, Jr., in *Equality Practice: Civil Unions and the Future of Gay Rights* (New York: Routledge, 2002), introduces the terms "politics of preservation" and the "politics of recognition" in his prologue (xi–xii).

4. Robert H. Knight, "How Domestic Partnerships and 'Gay Marriage' Threaten the Family," in *Same-Sex Marriage: The Moral and Legal Debate,* ed. Robert M. Baird and Stuart E. Rosenbaum (Amherst, N.Y.: Prometheus Books, 1997), 114.

5. Ibid., 115.

6. Robert H. Knight, *The Importance of Families and Marriage: Testimony of Robert H. Knight before the Senate Health, Education and Social Services Committee, State of Alaska regarding SB 308, Which Would Amend the State's Marriage Statute, March 18, 1996,* Equal Rights in Covenant Life 7 (Cleveland: United Church Board for Homeland Ministries, 1998), 1.

7. Knight, "How Domestic Partnerships and 'Gay Marriage' Threaten the Family," 108.

8. Ibid., 109.

9. Knight, "The Importance of Families and Marriage," 2.

10. John M. Finnis, "Law, Morality, and 'Sexual Orientation,'" *Notre Dame Law Review* 69, no. 5 (1994): 1064.

11. Ibid., 1062.

12. Ibid., 1066.

13. Ibid., 1068, n. 51.

14. Ibid., 1066–67.

15. Max L. Stackhouse, "The Prophetic Stand of the Ecumenical Churches on Homosexuality," in *Sexual Orientation and Human Rights in American Religious Discourse,* ed. Saul M. Olyan and Martha C. Nussbaum (New York: Oxford University Press, 1998), 121.

16. Ibid., 121–22.

17. Max L. Stackhouse, "The Heterosexual Norm," in *Homosexuality and Christian Community,* ed. Choon-Leong Seow (Louisville: Westminster John Knox Press, 1996), 141.

18. Stanley J. Grenz, *Welcoming but Not Affirming: An Evangelical Response to Homosexuality* (Louisville: Westminster John Knox Press, 1998), 115.

19. Ibid., 140–41.

20. Ibid., 141.

21. Ibid., 111.

22. Ibid., 112.

23. Ibid., 113.

24. Gay men's freedom *from* marriage also causes them to be envied, especially by heterosexual men who project onto their gay male counterparts their own deep fears of and fascination with uninhibited sexual license. As chapter 4 discusses, some LBGT marriage advocates use this argument about "uncivilized" gay men and the supposed excessive character of gay sex to justify making marriage available to gay men in order to "tame" them and rein in their sexuality, a point that early Christian and Reformation theologians might have appreciated, at least in terms of marriage as a means of sexual control.

25. Stanley Kurtz, "Listening Attentively: Ideas Have Consequences," *National Review* Online, August 8, 2001, www.nationalreview.com/contributors/kurtzprint080801 .html.

26. For a recent call to shift from "homosexualizing" HIV/AIDS to placing the pandemic in global perspective with its race, gender, and class implications, see Mary E. Hunt, "AIDS in a Globalized Economy: A Religious Reality Check," in *Body and Soul: Rethinking Sexuality as Justice-Love,* ed. Marvin M. Ellison and Sylvia Thorson-Smith (Cleveland: Pilgrim Press, 2003), 251–65.

27. Suzanne Pharr writes, "It is common knowledge that the majority of perpetrators of sexual abuse of children are heterosexual men," but the religious Right uses a strategy of disinformation in order to link gayness with abuse of children and thereby defame particularly gay men and discredit the movement for LBGT rights. In exploring "why the lie works," Pharr cites several reasons. First, many people fail to comprehend that rape and child sexual abuse are about power and control rather than sexual gratification. Second, confusion persists in conflating sexual acts with sexual orientation. Third, the refusal to accept the fact that the vast majority of child abusers are family members or trusted individuals helps sustain the myth that the "homosexual stranger" is the greatest threat and, therefore, "we leave our children even more vulnerable to abuse and undefended by those responsible for their well being" ("Pedophilia and the Endangerment of Children: How Wrong Can the Right Be?" *Transformation* 8, no. 3 [May–June 1993]: 2–3).

28. Stackhouse, "The Prophetic Stand of the Ecumenical Churches on Homosexuality," 125.

29. Ibid., 119.

30. Ibid., 120.

31. Ibid., 119.

32. Ibid., 120.

33. Grenz, *Welcoming but Not Affirming,* 153.

34. Ibid., 157.

35. Richard D. Mohr, "The Case for Gay Marriage," in *Morals, Marriage, and Parenthood: An Introduction to Family Ethics,* ed. Laurence D. Houlgate (Belmont, Calif.: Wadsworth, 1999), 83.

36. Elizabeth Janeway, *Man's World, Woman's Place: A Study in Social Mythology* (New York: Morrow, 1971).

37. Rosemary Radford Ruether, *Christianity and the Making of the Modern Family* (Boston: Beacon Press, 2000), 168.

38. For some of this early literature, see Susan Schechter, *Women and Male Violence: The Visions and Struggles of the Battered Women's Movement* (Boston: South End Press, 1982); Del Martin, *Battered Wives* (San Francisco: Glide Publications, 1976); and Marie M. Fortune, *Sexual Violence: The Unmentionable Sin* (New York: Pilgrim Press, 1986).

39. For a more extended analysis of the eroticization of injustice, see Marvin M. Ellison, *Erotic Justice: A Liberating Ethic of Sexuality* (Louisville: Westminster John Knox Press, 1996).

40. Susan Moller Okin, "Sexual Orientation and Gender: Dichotomizing Differences," in *Sex, Preference, and Family: Essays on Law and Nature*, ed. David M. Estlund and Martha C. Nussbaum (New York: Oxford University Press, 1997), 53.

41. Cheshire Calhoun (*Feminism, the Family, and the Politics of the Closet: Lesbian and Gay Displacement* [Oxford: Oxford University Press, 2000]) argues that cultural disrespect of gay men and lesbians is communicated largely through stereotypes that depict them as immoral rather than inferior: "While racial and gender discrimination are largely predicated on *inferiorizing* stereotypes, sexuality discrimination is largely predicated on *immoralizing* stereotypes whose ultimate suggestion is not that gay men and lesbians are *incompetent*, but that they are *untrustworthy* members of civil society" (105, her emphasis).

42. Jonathan Rauch, "Who's More Worthy? More Rauch vs. Kurtz on Gay Same-sex Marriage," guest comment on *National Review* Online, August 6, 2001, www.nationalreview.com/comment/comment-rauchprint080601.html.

43. Kath Weston, *Families We Choose: Lesbians, Gays, Kinship* (New York: Columbia University Press, 1991); *Our Families, Our Values: Snapshots of Queer Kinship*, ed. Robert E. Goss and Amy Adams Squire Strongheart (New York: Harrington Park Press, 1997); and Jeffrey Weeks, Brian Heaphy, and Catherine Donovan, *Same-Sex Intimacies: Families of Choice and Other Life Experiments* (New York: Routledge, 2001).

44. Rauch, "Who's More Worthy?" 3.

45. Charlotte J. Patterson, "Lesbian and Gay Parenting," APA Public Interest, American Psychological Association, APA Online, 1995, www.apa.org/pi/parent/html.

46. Ibid.

47. Ibid.

48. Ibid.

49. Michael Wald, "Same-Sex Couples: Marriage, Families, and Children: Same-Sex Couples Marriages and Family Policy," www.law.stanford.edu/faculty/wald/contents.shtml.

50. Franklin E. Kameny, "Gay Is Good," in *The Same Sex: An Appraisal of Homosexuality*, ed. Ralph W. Weltge (Philadelphia: Pilgrim Press, 1969), 131–32.

51. Ruether, *Christianity and the Making of the Modern Family*, 4.

52. Ibid., 7.

53. Ibid., 35.

54. E. J. Graff, *What Is Marriage For? The Strange Social History of Our Most Intimate Institution* (Boston: Beacon Press, 1999), 252.

55. Daniel Maguire, "The Morality of Homosexual Marriage," in *Same-Sex Marriage: The Moral and Legal Debate*, ed. Robert M. Baird and Stuart E. Rosenbaum (Amherst, N.Y.: Prometheus Books, 1997), 62.

56. Ibid., 63–64.

57. Ibid., 59.

58. *Baker v. Vermont* (filed December 20, 1999), 6, cited on the web page of Gay and Lesbian Advocates and Defenders, www.glad.org.

59. Ibid.

60. Ibid.

61. As Yuval Merin points out in *Equality for Same-Sex Couples: The Legal Recognition of Gay Partnerships in Europe and the United States* (Chicago: University of Chicago Press, 2002), some inequality may be legally and morally justified. For example, in order to correct patterns of gender injustice that have accumulated over time, women as a group may need preferential treatment in order "to further the special needs of women and redress past discrimination based on gender" (285). For an extended ethical analysis of affirmative action, see Daniel C. Maguire, *A New American Justice: Ending the White Male Monopolies* (Garden City, N.Y.: Doubleday, 1980).

62. David L. Chambers, "Couples: Marriage, Civil Union, and Domestic Partnership," in *Creating Change: Sexuality, Public Policy, and Civil Rights,* ed. John D'Emilio, William B. Turner, and Urvashi Vaid (New York: St. Martin's Press, 2000), 304.

63. James B. Nelson, *Embodiment: An Approach to Sexuality and Christian Theology* (Minneapolis: Augsburg, 1978), 207–9. In later writings, Nelson cites historian John Boswell's research and acknowledges "there is some emerging evidence that unions of gay and lesbian Christians were celebrated in some Christian churches far earlier than heterosexual marriages." See James B. Nelson, *Relationships: Blessed and Blessing, Equal Rights in Covenant Life* 7 (Cleveland: United Church Board for Homeland Ministries, 1998), 3.

Chapter Four / Marriage Advocates

1. Ellen Lewin, *Recognizing Ourselves: Ceremonies of Lesbian and Gay Commitment* (New York: Columbia University Press, 1998), 25.

2. Jack Rogers, "Same-Sex Marriage: Schloming Memorial Lectureship," *More Light Update* 21, no. 2 (November–December 2000), 7, 8.

3. *Economist,* January 6, 1996, 13–14, 68–70.

4. Patricia Smith, "Are Family Values Enduring Values?" in *Morals, Marriage, and Parenthood: An Introduction to Family Ethics,* ed. Laurence D. Houlgate (Belmont, Calif.: Wadsworth, 1999), 126.

5. Ibid.

6. Jeffrey Weeks, Brian Heaphy, and Catherine Donovan, *Same-Sex Intimacies: Families of Choice and Other Life Experiments* (London and New York: Routledge, 2001), 24. Don S. Browning in *Marriage and Modernization* (Grand Rapids, Mich.: William B. Eerdmans, 2003) speaks similarly of "critical familism" and a "critical marriage culture," concepts which signify equal-regard marriage and family patterns built on mutual respect, care, and distribution of goods and power (44–45). By and large, Browning skirts the issue of same-sex marriage. As Peter Steinfels writes in the *New York Times*, "Much of Professor Browning's project [Religion, Culture, and the Family] seems to weigh against same-sex marriage, without being entirely or explicitly closed to the possibility, especially if children are involved" (June 21, 2003, A16). See also Don Browning, Bonnie Miller-McLemore, Pamela Couture, Bernie Lyon, and Robert Franklin, *From Culture Wars to Common Ground* (Louisville: Westminster John Knox Press, 1997).

7. Ibid., their emphasis. Weeks and his colleagues also observe an interest in finding balance between individual satisfaction and mutual involvement in coupled relationships. They conclude that the quest for new forms of intimacy based on mutual respect and shared power does not portend "the collapse of the family, nor is it the triumph of unfettered hedonism. It is, we believe, the search for a new form of 'emotional democracy.'" This quest exists, as well, among many heterosexual couples, a point of commonality among those with a more mature understanding of what contemporary partnership requires (25).

8. Jonathan Rauch, "Who's More Worthy?" guest column on *National Review Online*, August 6, 2001, www.nationalreview.com.

9. Andrew Sullivan, "Liberation," *New Republic*, May 6, 1996, 2.

10. Andrew Sullivan, *Virtually Normal: An Argument about Homosexuality* (New York: Knopf, 1995), 185. Sullivan makes no qualification to this assertion, which puzzles and angers others within the LBGT community who grapple with a wide range of injustices and challenges, only one of which is lack of state recognition of their families.

11. Martha Nussbaum, *Sex and Social Justice* (New York: Oxford University Press, 1999), 203.

12. Ibid., 202, 203.

13. *Our Families, Our Values: Snapshots of Queer Kinship*, ed. Robert E. Goss and Amy Adams Squire Strongheart (New York: Harrington Park Press, 1997), xviii.

14. Ellen Lewin, "'You'll Never Walk Alone: Lesbian and Gay Weddings and the Authenticity of the Same-Sex Couple,'" in *Inside the American Couple: New Thinking, New Challenges*, ed. Marilyn Yalom and Laura L. Carstensen (Berkeley: University of California Press, 2002), 87.

15. Evan Wolfson, "All Together Now," *Advocate*, September 11, 2001, 34.

16. Robert Williams, "Toward a Theology for Lesbian and Gay Marriage," *Anglican Theological Review* 72, no. 2, 135. His emphasis.

17. Carlos A. Ball, *The Morality of Gay Rights: An Exploration in Political Philosophy* (New York: Routledge, 2003), 105.

18. Ibid., 88.

19. *Baker v. Vermont* (Docket no. 98-032), 44–45, cited on the web page of Gay and Lesbian Advocates and Defenders, www.glad.org/98-032A.op.

20. GLAD, "Why Marriage Matters" (Boston: Gay and Lesbian Advocates and Defenders, n.d.), 2.

21. Michael Wald, "Same-Sex Couples: Marriage, Families, and Children, Why Does the State Provide for and Regulate Marriage," www.law.stanford.edu/faculty/wald.

22. Rebecca Alpert, "Religious Liberty, Same-Sex Marriage, and the Case of Reconstructionist Judaism," in *God Forbid: Religion and Sex in American Public Life*, ed. Kathleen M. Sands (Oxford and New York: Oxford University Press, 2000), 125. The discussion in this section is informed by Alpert's analysis.

23. Ibid., 128–29.

24. Karen Lebacqz, "Expert Testimony on Holy Unions for the UMC Clergy Committee on Investigations," February 2000, www.psr.edu/page.cfm?l=62&id=91.

25. Ibid.

26. Jonathan Rauch, "Marriage for All," guest column on *National Review* Online, April 10, 2001, www.nationalreview.com.

27. Wald, "Same-Sex Couples: Marriage, Families, and Children."

28. William N. Eskridge, Jr., "The History of Same-Sex Marriage," *Virginia Law Review* 79, no. 7: 1442, 1485.

29. Anna Quindlen, "Getting Rid of the Sex Police," *Newsweek*, January 13, 2003, 72.

30. Carlos A. Ball, "That We Are Human, We Have Rights," *Gay and Lesbian Review/Worldwide* 9, no. 6 (November–December 2002): 32.

31. GLAD, "Civil Marriage for Same-Sex Couples: The Facts" (Boston: Gay and Lesbian Advocates and Defenders, August 2002), 25. Online see www.glad.org/Publications/CivilRightProject/CivilMarriage_TheFacts.PDF.

32. Yuval Merin, *Equality for Same-Sex Couples: The Legal Recognition of Gay Partnerships in Europe and the United States* (Chicago: University of Chicago Press, 2002), 278–79. His emphasis.

33. Williams, "Toward a Theology for Lesbian and Gay Marriage," 137.

34. The Editors, "Separate but Equal?" *New Republic Online*, January 10, 2000.

35. J. Michael Clark, *Doing the Work of Love: Men and Commitment in Same-Sex Couples* (Harriman, Tenn.: Men's Studies Press, 1999).

36. Nan D. Hunter, "Marriage, Law and Gender: A Feminist Inquiry," in *Sex Wars: Sexual Dissent and Political Culture*, ed. Lisa Duggan and Nan D. Hunter (New York: Routledge, 1995), 112.

37. William N. Eskridge, Jr., *Equality Practice: Civil Unions and the Future of Gay Rights* (New York: Routledge, 2002), 132.

38. Judy Grahn, "Flaming without Burning: Some of the Roles of Gay People in Society," cited in Williams, "Toward a Theology for Lesbian and Gay Marriage," 143.

39. Audre Lorde, "Man Child: A Black Lesbian Feminist's Response," in *Sister Outsider: Essays and Speeches by Audre Lorde* (Trumansburg, N.Y.: Crossing Press, 1984), 80.

40. GLAD, "Civil Marriage for Same-Sex Couple: The Facts," 33.

41. William N. Eskridge, Jr., *The Case for Same-Sex Marriage: From Sexual Liberty to Civilized Commitment* (New York: Free Press, 1996), 8 and 9.

42. Ibid., 9.

43. Ibid., 58.

44. Ibid., 84.

45. Martha Minow, *Making All the Difference: Inclusion, Exclusion, and American Law* (Ithaca, N.Y.: Cornell University Press, 1990), 20.

46. Ibid., 169.

47. Nussbaum, *Sex and Social Justice*, 185.

Chapter Five / Marriage Critics

1. Alisa Solomon, "Get Married? Yes, but Not by the State," *Village Voice*, January 9, 1996, 29.

2. The Editors, "Gay Marriage: A Must or a Bust?" *Out/Look* 2, no. 2 (Fall 1989): 8.

3. Janet Jakobsen and Ann Pellegrini, *Love the Sin: Sexual Regulation and the Limits of Religious Tolerance* (New York: New York University Press, 2003), 75, 91.

4. Ibid., 130.

5. Claudia Card, "Against Marriage and Motherhood," *Hypatia* 11, no. 3 (Summer 1996): 20, 14.

6. Michael Warner, "Normal and Normaller: Beyond Gay Marriage," *GLQ: The Journal of Gay and Lesbian Studies* 5, no. 2 (1999): 119–20.

7. Jakobsen and Pellegrini frame the dilemma this way: "How then [is it possible] to resist and challenge exclusion and at the same time change the terms of inclusion?" (Jakobsen and Pellegrini, *Love the Sin,* 149).

8. Warner, "Normal and Normaller," 120–21.

9. Ibid., 122.

10. Mary E. Hunt, "You Do, I Don't," in *Redefining Sexual Ethics: A Sourcebook of Essays, Stories, and Poems,* ed. Susan E. Davies and Eleanor H. Haney (Cleveland: Pilgrim Press, 1991), 254.

11. Paula Ettelbrick, "Since When Is Marriage a Path to Liberation?" in *Same-Sex Marriage: Pro and Con, A Reader,* ed. Andrew Sullivan (New York: Vintage Books, 1997), 118–24.

12. Ibid., 119. My emphasis.

13. Card, "Against Marriage," 10.

14. Ibid., 11.

15. Ibid. On the matter of domestic abuse, see my essay, "Setting the Captives Free: Same-Sex Domestic Violence and the Justice-Loving" in *Body and Soul: Rethinking Sexuality as Justice-Love,* ed. Marvin M. Ellison and Sylvia Thorson-Smith (Cleveland: Pilgrim Press, 2003), 284–99.

16. Nancy D. Polikoff, "We Will Get What We Ask For: Why Legalizing Gay and Lesbian Marriage Will Not 'Dismantle the Legal Structure of Gender in Every Marriage,'" *Virginia Law Review* 79, no. 7 (1993): 1538, 1537.

17. Solomon, "Get Married?" 29.

18. Jeffrey Weeks, Brian Heaphy, and Catherine Donovan, *Same-Sex Intimacies: Families of Choice and Other Life Experiments* (London and New York: Routledge, 2001), 89.

19. E. J. Graff, "Retying the Knot," in *Same-Sex Marriage: Pro and Con,* 138.

20. Warner, "Normal and Normaller," 128.

21. Jakobsen and Pellegrini, *Love the Sin,* 105.

22. Weeks, Heaphy, and Donovan, *Same-Sex Intimacies,* 19.

23. Michael Warner, *The Trouble with Normal: Sex, Politics, and the Ethics of Queer Life* (New York: Free Press, 1999), 82.

24. Ibid.

25. Jakobsen and Pellegrini, *Love the Sin,* 121.

26. Ibid.

27. Card, "Against Marriage," 8.

28. Nan D. Hunter, "Marriage, Law and Gender: A Feminist Inquiry," in *Sex Wars: Sexual Dissent and Political Culture,* ed. Lisa Duggan and Nan D. Hunter (London and New York: Routledge, 1995), 120.

29. Polikoff, "We Will Get What We Ask For," 1545.

30. Ettelbrick, "Since When Is Marriage a Path to Liberation?" *Out/Look* 2, no. 2 (Fall 1989): 14.

31. Chai R. Feldblum writes, "Unless we deal positively with the moral legitimacy of desiring and engaging in such sex, we may win a few battles along the way to gay

equality, but we will lose the ultimate war of complete and true equality" ("Keep the Sex in Same-Sex Marriage," *Harvard Gay and Lesbian Review* 4, no. 4 [Fall 1997]: 23).

32. Warner, *The Trouble with Normal*, 36 and 39.

33. Michael Bronski, *The Pleasure Principle: Sex, Backlash, and the Struggle for Gay Freedom* (New York: St. Martin's Press, 1998), 9. These more flexible norms include less rigid gender roles, more freedom for sexual experimentation even within committed relationships, family units that are self-defined and freely chosen rather than biologically defined and given, and alternative patterns of parenting.

34. Hunt, "You Do, I Don't," 256.

35. Weeks, Heaphy, and Donovan, *Same-Sex Intimacies*, 23.

36. Hunter, "Marriage, Law and Gender," 112.

37. Ibid., 120.

38. Anna Quindlen, quoted by Christine Pierce, "Gay Marriage," in *Same-Sex Marriage: The Moral and Legal Debate*, ed. Robert M. Baird and Stuart E. Rosenbaum (Amherst, N.Y.: Prometheus Books, 1997), 171.

39. Evan Wolfson, "Crossing the Threshold: Equal Marriage Rights for Lesbians and Gay Men and the Intra-Community Critique," *New York University Review of Law and Social Change* 21 (1994–95): 580, 590.

40. Pierce, "Gay Marriage," 176.

41. Pierce cites Justice Byron White's ruling in the 1986 *Bowers v. Hardwick* U.S. Supreme Court decision to the effect that "no connection between family, marriage, or procreation on the one hand and homosexual activity on the other has been demonstrated." As Pierce reads this ruling, she concludes that the majority on the Court failed to see that gay people have family relationships or intimate partnerships (175).

42. Warner, *The Trouble with Normal*, 1.

43. See Beverly Wildung, Harrison, *Making the Connections: Essays in Feminist Social Ethics*, ed. Carol S. Robb (Boston: Beacon Press, 1985), especially "Sexuality and Social Policy," 83–114.

44. Martha C. Nussbaum, "Experiments in Living," *New Republic Online*, January 3, 2000, www.tnr.com.

45. Ibid.

46. Warner, *The Trouble with Normal*, 123.

47. J. Michael Clark, *Doing the Work of Love: Men and Commitment in Same-Sex Couples* (Harriman, Tenn.: Men's Studies Press, 1999), 38–39.

48. Weeks, Heaphy, and Donovan, *Same-Sex Intimacies*, 11.

49. Ellen Lewin, " 'You'll Never Walk Alone': Lesbian and Gay Weddings and the Authenticity of the Same-Sex Couple," in *Inside the American Couple: New Thinking, New Challenges*, ed. Marilyn Yalom and Laura L. Carstensen (Berkeley: University of California Press, 2002), 104. See also Ellen Lewin, *Recognizing Ourselves: Ceremonies of Lesbian and Gay Commitment* (New York: Columbia University Press, 1998).

50. Yuval Merin, *Equality for Same-Sex Couples: The Legal Recognition of Gay Partnerships in Europe and the United States* (Chicago: University of Chicago Press, 2002), 302.

51. Morris B. Kaplan, *Sexual Justice: Democratic Citizenship and the Politics of Desire* (New York: Routledge, 1997), 227–35.

Chapter Six / Contested Christian Teaching

1. Mary Hunt, "What Makes for Good Sex? A Farewell to Easy Answers," *The Witness*, April 2000, www.thewitness.org/archive/april2000/hunt.goodsex.html.

2. Elizabeth Janeway, *Powers of the Weak* (New York: Morrow Quill Paperbacks, 1981), esp. 168–85.

3. For narratives of heterosexual allies, see *Called Out With: Stories of Solidarity*, ed. Sylvia Thorson-Smith et al. (Louisville: Westminster John Knox Press, 1997).

4. For one Christian ethicist's public appreciation for the LBGT community and its moral wisdom, see James B. Nelson, *Body Theology* (Louisville: Westminster John Knox Press, 1992), esp. chaps. 2, 4, and 12.

5. Michael Bronski, *The Pleasure Principle: Sex, Backlash, and the Struggle for Gay Freedom* (New York: St. Martin's Press, 1998), 242–43, 249.

6. On the limits of tolerance as a response to injustice, see Janet R. Jakobsen and Ann Pellegrini, *Love the Sin: Sexual Regulation and the Limits of Religious Tolerance* (New York: New York University Press, 2003).

7. William N. Eskridge, Jr., *The Case for Same-Sex Marriage: From Sexual Liberty to Civilized Commitment* (New York: Free Press, 1996), 183–84.

8. Gayle S. Rubin, "Thinking Sex: Notes for a Radical Theory of the Politics of Sexuality," in *The Lesbian and Gay Studies Reader*, ed. Henry Abelove, Michele Aina Barale, and David M. Halperin (New York: Routledge, 1993), 15.

9. Carter Heyward, *Touching Our Strength: The Erotic as Power and the Love of God* (San Francisco: Harper & Row, 1989), 4.

10. Judith Plaskow, "Toward a New Theology of Sexuality," in *Redefining Sexual Ethics: A Sourcebook of Essays, Stories, and Poems*, ed. Susan E. Davies and Eleanor H. Haney (Cleveland: Pilgrim Press, 1991), 309–19. Also, Judith Plaskow, *Standing Again at Sinai: Judaism from a Feminist Perspective* (San Francisco: Harper & Row, 1990), esp. 170–210.

11. Samuel Laeuchli, *Power and Sexuality: The Emergence of Canon Law at the Synod of Elvira* (Philadelphia: Temple University Press, 1972); and Mark D. Jordan, *The Invention of Sodom in Christian Theology* (Chicago: University of Chicago Press, 1997).

12. Beverly Wildung Harrison, *Making the Connections: Essays in Feminist Social Ethics*, ed. Carol S. Robb (Boston: Beacon Press, 1985), 138.

13. The phrase is Gayle Rubin's from "Thinking Sex: Notes for a Radical Theory of the Politics of Sexuality," 11.

14. Mark D. Jordan, *The Ethics of Sex* (Malden, Mass.: Blackwell Publishers, 2002), 1.

15. Ibid., 124–25.

16. Ibid., 123–24. Sadly, most Christians do not know that theirs is a tradition with some extraordinary erotic literature, not only from the mystics but also in the Bible. On this score alone, the Song of Songs is worth a read. For commentary, see Renita J. Weems, "Song of Songs," in *The Women's Bible Commentary*, ed. Carol A. Newsom and Sharon H. Ringe (Louisville: Westminster John Knox Press, 1992); Phyllis Trible, *God and the Rhetoric of Sexuality* (Philadelphia: Fortress Press, 1978); Gary Comstock, *Gay Theology without Apology* (Cleveland: Pilgrim Press, 1993); and Marvin M. Ellison, *Erotic Justice: A Liberating Ethic of Sexuality* (Louisville: Westminster John Knox Press, 1996), esp. 70–75.

17. Ibid., 155.

18. Ibid., 112.

19. Ibid., 113.

20. Ibid., 117.

21. Rosemary Radford Ruether, *Christianity and the Making of the Modern Family* (Boston: Beacon Press, 2000), 74.

22. Ibid., 78.

23. The religious literature on sexual and domestic abuse, as well as clergy abuse, has become quite voluminous. For earlier and still influential writings, see Marie Marshall Fortune, *Sexual Violence: The Unmentionable Sin, An Ethical and Pastoral Perspective* (New York: Pilgrim Press, 1983); Marie M. Fortune, *Keeping the Faith: Guidance for Christian Women Facing Abuse* (San Francisco: Harper, 1987); Marie M. Fortune, *Is Nothing Sacred? When Sex Invades the Pastoral Relationship* (San Francisco: Harper & Row, 1989); Karen Lebacqz and Ronald G. Barton, *Sex in the Parish* (Louisville: Westminster John Knox Press, 1991); and *Boundary Wars: Intimacy and Distance in Healing Relationships*, ed. Katherine Hancock Ragsdale (Cleveland: Pilgrim Press, 1996).

24. The feminist theological literature on sexuality, pleasure, and erotic empowerment is also expansive. For some of the pioneering work, see Carter Heyward, *Our Passion for Justice: Images of Power, Sexuality, and Liberation* (New York: Pilgrim Press, 1984); Carter Heyward, *Touching Our Strength: The Erotic as Power and the Love of God* (San Francisco: Harper & Row, 1989); Beverly Wildung Harrison, *Making the Connections: Essays in Feminist Social Ethics*, ed. Carol S. Robb (Boston: Beacon Press, 1985); Judith Plaskow, "Toward a New Theology of Sexuality," in *Standing Again at Sinai* (San Francisco: Harper & Row, 1991); Mary D. Pellauer, "The Moral Significance of Female Orgasm: Toward Sexual Ethics That Celebrates Women's Sexuality," *Journal of Feminist Studies in Religion* 9, nos. 1–2 (Spring/Fall 1993): 161–82; Christine E. Gudorf, *Body, Sex, and Pleasure: Reconstructing Christian Sexual Ethics* (Cleveland: Pilgrim Press, 1994); Marvin M. Ellison, *Erotic Justice*; Patricia Beattie Jung, Mary E. Hunt, and Radhika Balakrishnan, eds., *Good Sex: Feminist Perspectives from the World's Religions* (New Brunswick, N.J.: Rutgers University Press, 2001); Kelly Brown Douglas, *Sexuality and the Black Church* (Maryknoll, N.Y.: Orbis, 1999); J. Michael Clark, *Doing the Work of Love: Men and Commitment in Same-Sex Couples* (Harriman, Tenn.: Men's Studies Press, 1999); and *Body and Soul: Rethinking Sexuality as Justice-Love*, ed. Marvin M. Ellison and Sylvia Thorson-Smith (Cleveland: Pilgrim Press, 2003), esp. Robert E. Goss, "Gay Erotic Spirituality and the Recovery of Sexual Pleasure," 201–17.

25. John Shelby Spong, *Living in Sin? A Bishop Rethinks Sexuality* (San Francisco: Harper & Row, 1988), esp. chap. 12, "Betrothal: An Idea Whose Time Has Come," 177–87.

26. Adrian Thatcher, *Living Together and Christian Ethics* (New York: Cambridge University Press, 2002), 218.

27. Adrian Thatcher, *Marriage after Modernity: Christian Marriage in Postmodern Times* (Sheffield, U.K.: Sheffield Academic Press, 1999), 112.

28. Ibid., 131.

29. Aquinas is quoted in Rita Brock, "Marriage Troubles," in *Body and Soul: Rethinking Sexuality as Justice-Love*, ed. Marvin M. Ellison and Sylvia Thorson-Smith (Cleveland: Pilgrim Press, 2003), 352.

30. Ibid.

31. Mark Jordan observes that Christianity "has manufactured and distributed a number of sexual identities — the Virgin Martyr, the Pure Priest, the Witch, the Sodomite" (*The Ethics of Sex,* 15). To this list I would add the contemporary image of the bona fide heterosexual who is certified as such by entrance into marriage.

32. Shel Silverstein's children's books, including *The Giving Tree* (New York: HarperCollins Publishers, 1999) and *The Missing Piece* (New York: HarperCollins Publishers, 1976) reinforce this cultural notion for readers at an early age.

33. Christine E. Gudorf in *Body, Sex, and Pleasure: Reconstructing Christian Sexual Ethics* (Cleveland: Pilgrim Press, 1994) notes that Christian sexual mores are legalistic, rule-bound, punitive, and outdated. The church's code has been based on faulty notions of the human person and on prescientific understandings of biology, reproduction, and human development. She suggests that just as the Dutch Reformed Church of South Africa has had to repudiate its traditional teaching on racial apartheid, so now "the same kind of renunciation of traditional teaching in sexuality, followed by repentance, is necessary on the part of all Christian churches today in response to the suffering and victimization it has long supported and legitimated" (2).

34. On the link between body alienation and disconnection from the earth, see J. Michael Clark, *Beyond Our Ghettos: Gay Theology in Ecological Perspective* (Cleveland: Pilgrim Press, 1993); Daniel T. Spencer, *Gay and Gaia: Ethics, Ecology and the Erotic* (Cleveland: Pilgrim Press, 1996); and Daniel T. Spencer, "Keeping Body, Soul, and Earth Together: Revisioning Justice-Love as an Ecological Ethic of Right Relation," in *Body and Soul: Rethinking Sexuality as Justice-Love,* ed. Marvin M. Ellison and Sylvia Thorson-Smith (Cleveland: Pilgrim Press, 2003), 319–33.

35. For diverse voices on religion, sexuality, and sexual ethics, see *Body and Soul.*

36. James B. Nelson writes, "Sexuality, most broadly and richly interpreted, is the divinely given energy for connection." Nelson, "Introduction," *Sexuality and the Sacred: Sources for Theological Reflection,* ed. James B. Nelson and Sandra P. Longfellow (Louisville: Westminster John Knox Press, 1994), xvii.

37. For one proposal for reconstructing Christian sexual ethics, see Ellison, *Erotic Justice,* esp. "Reimagining Good Sex: The Eroticizing of Mutual Respect and Pleasure," 76–93.

38. On friendship and sexuality, see Carter Heyward, *Touching Our Strength: The Erotic as Power and the Love of God* (San Francisco: Harper & Row, 1989); Mary E. Hunt, *Fierce Tenderness: A Feminist Theology of Friendship* (New York: Crossroad, 1991); Elizabeth Stuart, *Just Good Friends: Towards a Lesbian and Gay Theology of Relationships* (London: Mowbray, 1994); and J. Michael Clark, *Doing the Work of Love: Men and Commitment in Same-Sex Relationships* (Harriman, Tenn.: Men's Studies Press, 1999).

39. Larry Rasmussen and Daniel C. Maguire, *Ethics for a Small Planet: New Horizons on Population, Consumption and Ecology* (Albany: State University of New York Press, 1988). See also Rasmussen's *Earth Community, Earth Ethics* (Maryknoll, N.Y.: Orbis Books, 1996), as well as Larry Rasmussen and Cynthia Moe-Lobeda, "The Reform Dynamic," in *The Promise of Lutheran Ethics,* ed. Karen Bloomquist and John Stumme (Minneapolis: Fortress Press, 1998), 131–50.

40. This is the thesis of Daniel C. Maguire's *The Moral Core of Judaism and Christianity: Reclaiming the Revolution* (Minneapolis: Fortress Press, 1993).

41. John B. Cobb, Jr., *Matters of Life and Death* (Louisville: Westminster John Knox Press, 1991), 97.

42. Ibid. Cobb stresses that the reversal on divorce is singularly noteworthy because the prohibition against divorce was not only commanded by the central authority of the Christian tradition, it also "appears at a far more central place than is the case with other doctrines on which many Protestants continue to appeal to Scripture as authoritative," including the scattered "texts of terror" used to discredit same-sex love (97).

43. Ibid.

44. Elisabeth Schüssler Fiorenza, *Bread Not Stone: The Challenge of Feminist Biblical Interpretation* (Boston: Beacon Press, 1984), esp. 36–42.

45. Jordan, *The Ethics of Sex*, 174.

Chapter Seven / Queer Notions

1. Sallie McFague, *Life Abundant: Rethinking Theology and Economy for a Planet in Peril* (Minneapolis: Fortress Press, 2001), 23.

2. Arlie Russell Hochschild, *The Second Shift: Working Parents and the Revolution at Home* (New York: Viking, 1989).

3. Adrian Thatcher, *Marriage after Modernity: Christian Marriage in Postmodern Times* (Sheffield, U.K.: Sheffield Academic Press, 1999), 9.

4. Judith Plaskow, "Decentering Sex: Rethinking Jewish Sexual Ethics," in *God Forbid: Religion and Sex in American Public Life*, ed. Kathleen M. Sands (New York: Oxford University Press, 2000), 23.

5. On the Right's well-funded campaign to destroy one Protestant denomination's legacy and established structures for justice ministries, see Leon Howell, *United Methodism @ Risk: A Wake-Up Call* (Kingston, N.Y.: Information Project for United Methodists, 2003). See also Lewis C. Daly, *A Moment to Decide: The Crisis in Mainstream Presbyterianism* (New York: Institute for Democracy Studies, 2000).

6. McFague, *Life Abundant*, 209.

7. Nancy D. Polikoff, "Why Lesbians and Gay Men Should Read Martha Fineman," *American University Journal of Gender, Social Policy and the Law* 8 (1999): 175.

8. On bisexuality and ethics, see Susan Halcomb Craig, "Bisexuality: Variations on a Theme," in *Body and Soul: Rethinking Sexuality as Justice-Love*, ed. Marvin M. Ellison and Sylvia Thorson-Smith (Cleveland: Pilgrim Press, 2003), 114–28.

9. The legal status of a transgender person's marriage has not been fully resolved in the courts. For persons who are married and then transition, their marriages remain valid, subject only to the wishes of both spouses to stay married. For persons who transition before they seek to marry, the practical reality is that their marriages may never be questioned unless an annulment is sought or a third party brings forward a legal challenge, such as questioning a surviving spouse's right to automatic inheritance. As legal advocates at Gay and Lesbian Advocates and Defenders (GLAD) contend, "Presumably, if a state permits an individual to legally change his or her sex, the person's new legal sex should be recognized for all purposes, including marriage." However, some court decisions have not ruled in favor of the marital rights of transgender people. See "GLAD Publications: Transgender Discrimination," 12–13, www.glad.org/publications.

10. Christine E. Gudorf, "The Erosion of Sexual Dimorphism: Challenges to Religion and Religious Ethics," *Journal of the American Academy of Religion* 69, no. 4

(December 2001): 881. See also Virginia Ramey Mollenkott, *Omnigender: A Trans-religious Approach* (Cleveland: Pilgrim Press, 2001) and "Crossing Gender Borders: Toward a New Paradigm," in *Body and Soul: Rethinking Sexuality as Justice-Love,* ed. Marvin M. Ellison and Sylvia Thorson-Smith (Cleveland: Pilgrim Press, 2003), 185–97.

11. William Julius Wilson, "Where Are We Going?" in *Marriage — Just a Piece of Paper?* ed. Katherine Anderson, Don Browning, and Brian Boyer (Grand Rapids, Mich.: William B. Eerdmans, 2002), 401, 405.

12. Martha A. Fineman, *The Autonomy Myth: A Theory of Dependency* (New York: Free Press, 2003), 105–8.

13. Ibid., 123.

14. For a national organization dedicated to promoting a diversity of family and relational options, see Alternatives to Marriage Project, P.O. Box 991010, Boston, MA 02199; www.unmarried.org.

15. Fineman, *The Autonomy Myth,* 135–36.

16. Stephen L. Carter, " 'Defending' Marriage: A Modest Proposal," *Howard Law Journal* 41 (Winter 1988): 216.

17. Ibid.

18. Ibid., 219.

19. Ibid., 225. If marriage returned to its originating religious home and was re-garded as a sacred pledge that unites two persons for life, Carter conjectures that even the high divorce rate might well be turned around. "My view of the divorce rate has always been that we don't have divorce rates so high because divorce is too easy. The divorce rate is so high because marriage is too easy" (225).

20. In fall 2000, a group of Protestant and Catholic religious leaders, including the general secretary of the liberal National Council of Churches of Christ in the USA, issued "A Christian Declaration on Marriage," which defines marriage as "a holy union of one man and one woman" entered into for a lifetime. Public controversy was sparked almost immediately after the statement was issued.

21. Juan M. C. Oliver, "Why Gay Marriage?" *Journal of Men's Studies* 4, no. 3 (February 1996): 214, 221. On the blessing of same-sex unions, see John Boswell, *Same-Sex Unions in Premodern Europe* (New York: Villard Books, 1994); James B. Nelson, *Relationships: Blessed and Blessing,* Equal Rights in Covenant Life 7 (Cleveland: United Church Board for Homeland Ministries, 1998); and Mary E. Hunt, "You Do, I Don't," in *Redefining Sexual Ethics: A Sourcebook of Essays, Stories, and Poems,* ed. Susan E. Davies and Eleanor H. Haney (Cleveland: Pilgrim Press, 1991), 253–57.

22. See Robert McAfee Brown, *Spirituality and Liberation: Overcoming the Great Fallacy* (Philadelphia: Westminster Press, 1988), esp. 97–108; and Daniel C. Maguire, *The Moral Core of Judaism and Christianity: Reclaiming the Revolution* (Minneapolis: Fortress Press, 1993), esp. 208–30. Maguire writes, "Justice, indeed, is the primary love-language of the Bible. Jesus was quite typical of his tradition in rarely speaking of 'love' " (128).

23. James Newton Poling, *Deliver Us from Evil* (Minneapolis: Fortress Press, 1996), 112.

24. Douglas John Hall, *The End of Christendom and the Future of Christianity* (Valley Forge, Pa.: Trinity Press International, 1997).

25. "Methodist Pastor Faces Trial for Uniting Two Men," *New York Times*, March 25, 1999, A18.

26. For sermons by pastors who have declared a marriage moratorium until full marriage rights (and responsibilities) are made equally available to same-sex couples, see F. Jay Deacon, "Desire! A Valentine's Sermon," at www.uunorthampton.org/sermons, and Fred Small, "Why Gay Marriage Matters," a sermon delivered at First Church Unitarian, Littleton, New Hampshire, February 2, 2003. See also "Statement on Inclusive Marriage" by the Session, Mount Auburn Presbyterian Church, Cincinnati, February 28, 2001, in *More Light Update* (Summer 2002): 15.

27. See Fineman, *The Myth of Autonomy*; and *Welfare Policy: Feminist Critiques*, ed. Elizabeth M. Bounds, Pamela K. Brubaker, and Mary E. Hobgood (Cleveland: Pilgrim Press, 1999).

28. E. B. Saunders, "Reformer's Choice: Marriage License or Just License?" from *ONE Magazine*, August 1953, reprinted in *Gay and Lesbian Review*, November–December 2001, 24.

29. Larry Rasmussen, "Creative Communities," in *Practicing Our Faith: A Way of Life for a Searching People*, ed. Dorothy C. Bass (San Francisco: Jossey-Bass Publishers, 1997), 125. In his discussion Rasmussen is drawing on Ronald Heifetz, *Leadership without Easy Answers* (Cambridge, Mass.: Belknap Press of Harvard University Press, 1994).

30. Sallie McFague, *Models of God: Theology for an Ecological, Nuclear Age* (Philadelphia: Fortress Press, 1987), 130.

31. Renita J. Weems, *Battered Love: Marriage, Sex, and Violence in the Hebrew Scriptures* (Minneapolis: Fortress Press, 1995).

32. On the liberating power of this image of an unmarried God, see Rita Brock, "Marriage Troubles," in *Body and Soul: Rethinking Sexuality as Justice-Love*, ed. Marvin M. Ellison and Sylvia Thorson-Smith (Cleveland: Pilgrim Press, 2003), 352–74.

33. On the unmarried Jesus, see Rosemary Radford Ruether, *Christianity and the Making of the Modern Family* (Boston: Beacon Press, 2000); Mark D. Jordan, *The Ethics of Sex* (Malden, Mass.: Blackwell Publishers, 2002); and William E. Phipps, *The Sexuality of Jesus* (Cleveland: Pilgrim Press, 1996).

34. Bill Lippert's statement is found in Linda Hollingdale, *Creating Civil Union: Opening Hearts and Minds* (Hinesburg, Vt.: Common Humanity Press, 2002), 164.

35. Patricia Hill Collins, *Black Feminist Thought: Knowledge, Consciousness, and the Politics of Empowerment* (New York: Routledge and Kegan Paul, 1991), 182.

Index